822.33 Powell, Raymond.

Shakespeare and the
critics' debate

1950

DATE			

SHAKESPEARE AND THE CRITICS' DEBATE

A Guide for Students

SHAKESPEARE AND THE CRITICS' DEBATE

RAYMOND POWELL

ROWMAN AND LITTLEFIELD
TOTOWA, NEW JERSEY

First published in the United States 1980 by
ROWMAN AND LITTLEFIELD, Totowa, N.J.

Library of Congress Cataloging in Publication Data

Powell, Raymond.
   Shakespeare and the critics' debate.

   Includes bibliographical references and index.
   1. Shakespeare, William, 1564–1616—Criticism and
Interpretation—History. 2. Shakespeare, William, 1564–
1616—Study and teaching. I. Title.
PR2965.P6 1980   822.3'3   79–23135
ISBN 0–8476–6227–6

Printed in Hong Kong

Contents

FOR MIRIAM

Preface

This book is an attempt to provide something I should have been glad of when I was a student. I had then a strong but uncertain sense of Shakespeare's greatness and a correspondingly uncertain sense of what kind of help I was likely to get as I thumbed the Shakespeare-criticism section of the library shelves. The impact of the plays was overwhelming; so too (though in a different way) was that of the critics; and behind it all lurked the suspicion that in the criticism of Shakespeare opinions were endlessly bandied about and there was no way of knowing who was right and who was wrong. Such reactions are no doubt not uncommon. There seemed something to be said for a guide to the different ways of approaching Shakespeare which also tried to deal with the fundamental problem – where under all that pile of books is Shakespeare himself?

How far I have succeeded in making sense of Shakespeare and his critics is for the reader to judge. I should, however, like to acknowledge the debts I have accumulated during the writing of this book: to John Wilders, who first helped me to give shape to the ideas on which it is based; to the Fellows and members of the Shakespeare Institute, University of Birmingham, England, where some of the ideas were sharpened during my tenure of a two-year Fellowship; for reading and commenting on the final draft, to Gabrielle Boole, Fred Inglis and my friends at Bulmershe College of Higher Education – Christine MacLeod, Dennis Butts, Geoff Harvey, Tony Watkins and David Williams; and, lastly, to my wife, without whose constant help and encouragement the book would probably never have been completed. Although conscious of shortcomings that remain, I am nevertheless grateful for the help that prevented many more.

All quotations from Shakespeare's plays are taken from *The Complete Works* edited by Peter Alexander (London and Glasgow, 1951).

RAYMOND POWELL

1 Literary Criticism and Shakespeare

Literary criticism is a paradoxical activity. From one point of view critics can be regarded, not altogether unfairly, as purveyors of opinion, endlessly contradicting each other and lacking either inclination or capacity to transform their conclusions into a significant body of knowledge. It may be further claimed that the twentieth century with its vast increase in critical studies has generated in the end as much heat as light and as much confusion as insight for the unwary student. Estragon in *Waiting for Godot* was even unkind enough to use 'critic' as the ultimate term of personal abuse. But by only a slight shift of emphasis these negative aspects of literary criticism can be converted into its chief source of strength. The fact that it produces no developing body of knowledge means that it promotes no orthodoxy. That it is a chorus of frequently inharmonious voices affirms the central truth that only in the individual response is literature kept alive. And the process whereby views are developed, changed and supplanted enacts the continuing attempt to understand and reinterpret the significance of great literature for each generation. Literary criticism is part of the finer consciousness of our culture; and, despite the routine productions that occasionally seem its most visible manifestation, it symbolises the enduring importance of literature. So at least it can be argued.

Normally we read a critic on Shakespeare because we hope for some insight into a play in which we are interested. The fact is, though, that, whatever that critic has to say, someone somewhere is sure to have produced a convincing argument for a quite contrary point of view. Critics disagree about other writers as well. But in this respect – the range, diversity and sheer contradictoriness of response that he provokes – Shakespeare must be pre-eminent. It is his most distinctive and fascinating quality, and it forms the starting-point for what follows.

I am interested in the contradictoriness of Shakespeare's critics because it is a means of shedding light on the inexhaustibility of his plays.

Except in passing I am not concerned to supply a 'Good Food Guide' directing the reader where to go in the feast of Shakespeare criticism before him: critic X is good on this play, critic Y is better on that, and so forth. So much has been written on Shakespeare by now that certain definable groupings of individual critics embodying common approaches naturally suggest themselves. They provide a convenient, even necessary, framework for the examination of the variety and contradictoriness of Shakespeare criticism. At the end of this chapter I shall summarise the various approaches, and the major ones will be considered in more detail in later chapters on individual plays. I shall be looking at these approaches partly to see in what different ways they nourish our understanding of Shakespeare's work and also to develop my investigation into the source of Shakespeare's inexhaustibility. To enliven the conventional metaphor, all so-called critical approaches are presumably concerned to reach or approach as close as possible to the essential Shakespeare. If one asks what or where the essential Shakespeare is, the answer must surely lie in Shakespeare's inexhaustibility, that feature of his work – whatever it is – which generates so many approaches and so many conflicting interpretations in the first place. I shall be using the critics and their divergent responses in order to describe what I take to be the underlying structure of Shakespeare's plays and the essential workings of his dramatic imagination.

There is a prior problem. The validity of such an investigation requires a minimum confidence in literary criticism as an intellectual discipline. We have to believe that literature can be discussed with some degree of objectivity. Consequently I must start by dealing with the charge glanced at in the opening paragraph – that literary criticism amounts to so much opinion-swapping. Before we can claim to be talking objectively about Shakespeare, certainly before we are entitled to invoke such a grand abstraction as 'the essential Shakespeare', we need to be sure that criticism is capable of objectivity at all.

I

Nothing renders literary criticism absurd faster than the suspicion that one man's interpretation of a work is democratically equal to that of his neighbour. But on what basis are we to discriminate between them? The solution to this traditional problem of literary criticism lies at one remove in the work of literature itself. Literary discussion, like any other form of discussion, implies that some *thing* is being discussed. If a work of literature has an objective existence separate from the endless subjective experiences of it, then discussion has something to appeal to, a basis on which to assess divergent interpretations. There are two main questions: what is the essential nature of a work of literature; and what degree of objectivity does it in fact possess?

The answer to both questions lies in the words of which the work is composed. Subjective assertions about what one feels or thinks about a work are validated by reference to the text. It supplies the necessary evidence in support or refutation of what he says. Words span the worlds of public and private experience, both making possible the experience of the work in the individual consciousness and guaranteeing its objective existence. They form common ground between writer and reader and between one reader and another. Words have generally accepted meanings. They are therefore public property. So something that is composed of words – such as a work of literature – is public property as well; and the discussion of it – literary criticism – has a minimum claim to be considered a rational activity.[1]

Nevertheless, to guarantee the objective public existence of a work of literature is one thing. It does not explain the well-grounded feeling that the work cannot be wholly objectified and externalised. It is sometimes possible to be clearly wrong about a work; errors of fact can be committed. This ought in principle to imply that one can also be right. But 'right', together with related terms such as 'true' and 'correct' which suggest not so much an interpretation of as a solution to a work of literature, are in practice never used. All kinds of alternatives are employed instead – 'perceptive', 'illuminating', 'helpful', 'persuasive'. It seems therefore that the words of a work of literature confer on it some kind of objective existence, but only up to a point.

The main reason why this is so is that to a limited extent words are for the writer what clay is for the sculptor. Writers are concerned not just with what words say but also with what they can be used to do: to build imaginary worlds; to create states of feeling; to arouse feelings; to offer either new insights or the emotional reality behind truths dulled by long acquaintance; to heighten our perceptions less by what we are told than by what we are directly shown. None of this is capable of being precisely quantified. A writer turns to his own account the fact (banal, but it is worth emphasising) that language is not used by a homogeneous mass of people in an identical way. Meaning in the fullest sense is determined by individual experience. Furthermore, language develops; meanings change; words are metaphorically, if not metaphysically, alive. So the language which the writer transforms in the act of writing is then subtly transformed again in the multitude of individual consciousnesses which will read and respond to it. But it is still the public language the writer uses, and this ensures that an irreducible minimum of meaning is communicated. However obscure a writer's work, whether in local detail or in total effect, there are always elements which, even if only at a primitive level, 'make sense'.

Public and private, objective and subjective – we are not only entitled, we are obliged, to have it both ways. The precise way the balance is struck in any given work will vary enormously: one thinks of a poem by Ben Jonson as against one, say, by Dylan Thomas. It follows, in general terms, that a totally objective account of a work of literature is impossible in principle; but it also follows that, because the writer makes use of the language of ordinary discourse, his work will always bear rational comment and discussion.

My argument is in essence a very simple one: that there is a limited but undeniable objectivity about a work of literature; that there is a similar limited but undeniable rationality to literary criticism; and that the latter is directly consequent on the former. Literary discussion is rational (up to a point), because it is a discussion of something that is objectively 'there' (again, up to a point).

Since this is all somewhat general, perhaps I can illustrate what I mean with two opposed readings of a short passage in *The Tempest*. At the end of the play Prospero, reconciling himself to those who have wronged him, addresses his treacherous brother, Antonio, thus:

> For you, most wicked sir, whom to call brother
> Would even infect my mouth, I do forgive
> Thy rankest fault – all of them; and require
> My dukedom of thee, which perforce I know
> Thou must restore.   (v i 130–4)

On one level the passage presents no problems of interpretation. The language is simple, and the meaning is clear. It is the tone that is elusive. What is the nature of the forgiveness that Prospero offers Antonio? In what spirit does he address his brother? Forgiveness which refuses to acknowledge kinship may seem a somewhat odd kind ('whom to call brother / Would even infect my mouth'). Derek Traversi thinks not so, and explains the speech as follows:

> Justice, based on the moral condemnation which is felt so strongly behind 'infect' and 'rankest' and in the bitter afterthought 'all of them', needs to be satisfied as well as love; even in the culminating moment of happiness the reality of sin is alive to the memory. Forgiveness and condemnation are fused in a single gesture.[2]

Bonamy Dobrée, on the other hand, is outraged by the speech, finds the tone repellent, and asks in obvious disbelief, 'Does that sound like forgiveness? Is that how you would speak to a man whom you love as you forgive him?'[3]

Well, forgiveness accompanied by the warmth of returning love it clearly is not. The central point, on which Dobrée and Traversi disagree, is whether it can be regarded as forgiveness at all. In Traversi's view it is forgiveness which refuses to blink those facts for which forgiveness is required. In order to assent to Traversi's reading we too must feel in Prospero's speech the presence of a heartfelt forgiveness accompanied by a condemnation of past sin which, while stern, is nevertheless impersonal. If we feel Prospero's words to contain a residue of personal rancour, of bile and resentment at the crime committed against him years ago, then his forgiveness exists in name only. My own view inclines more to Dobrée than Traversi, but I do not see how one could finally convince someone who took Traversi's view that he was wrong. In the theatre much would depend on the tone of voice in which the actor delivers the speech. But the very fact that it could be delivered in different ways leaves us no further forward in deciding which of the two critics has got it right.

My reason for drawing attention to this minor crux, as is probably clear, is not to resolve it but rather to demonstrate that it cannot be resolved. If we attend to what the words are doing here, we can go so far (quite a long way in fact) in deciding whether we agree with Dobrée or Traversi. But the words by themselves do not mediate the experience with that complete unambiguous clarity that would enable us to say definitely which reading is correct.

A further factor which influences the precise tone and weight that we attribute to Prospero's words is the interpretative context in which they are set. Just as even the finest line depends for its fullest effect upon its context, so too does the most banal. Even more so, in fact. The less distinguished the writing, the more we need the context. A character in a play who announces, 'It's raining', is presumably passing on information; whether he is also expressing pleasure, relief, disappointment, boredom or whatever, only the context will indicate. The way we take Prospero's words at this late stage in *The Tempest* depends in part on our impression of him built up in the previous part of the play. Dobrée sees Prospero as a rather crotchety old gentleman, and he interprets the speech, consistent with that view, as a very poor gesture at forgiveness. Traversi, on the other hand, regards Prospero throughout as the embodiment of civilised values, and he interprets the speech accordingly. The one view of Prospero's character slants the speech this way, the other that.

It must be added that somewhere in our interpretation of Prospero's character, and hence of this particular moment, there exists an element of pure subjectivity. However much we try to keep our eye on the object, our personal predilections are bound to intrude. Prospero is an authority figure. What we make of him is necessarily influenced by our attitudes to different kinds of authority – those, so far as *The Tempest* is concerned, of a schoolmaster, of a colonial governor, or of God. They affect the degree of admiration or otherwise that Prospero elicits from us. Although the play can guide and shape our attitude to him, we are not computers, and no work of literature can programme our response.

At one extreme lies the illusion of objectivity – the belief that we are discussing, reporting and commenting on, in Matthew Arnold's phrase, 'the object as in itself it really is'. At the other extreme lies uncontrolled subjectivity – using a work as a sounding board for our prejudices and hearing from it the gratifying sound of our own voices.

Treading a middle path is even more difficult with Shakespeare than it is with other writers, and what will help us to avoid both extremes is a readiness to talk about Shakespeare's intentions. This is, I realise, an unconventional recommendation. The arguments making up the so-called intentional fallacy[4] are well known: that we cannot ultimately know what were a writer's intentions; that a statement of intentions, if available, may or may not correspond to what he finally wrote; and that a knowledge of his intentions could not and should not preclude us from finding further meanings in what he has written. These objections are true but irrelevant. They correspond to the difficulties involved in all use of intentional language. Intentions are, by definition, matters of inference. With people in ordinary life we infer their intentions from their actions; with writers we infer theirs from what they write. A work of literature is not an *objet trouvé*; it possesses an intrinsic meaning put there by the author; and because the author put it there, we are entitled to talk about his intentions.

Some reference to Shakespeare's intentions is, however, more than a matter of permission; it is almost a positive duty. The slow and delicate business of teasing out what Shakespeare is doing, where he is leading us, what effects he is out to create, is an expression of that minimum humility which requires us to submit ourselves to the work instead of arrogantly requiring the work to submit itself to us. More to the point, the imaginative effort involved anchors us firmly in the work itself and thereby prevents the descent into subjectivity referred to above. At the same time common sense ensures that inferences about Shakespeare's intentions remain inferences; they cannot be offered as fact. Someone who is thus made aware of the problematic nature of interpretation is unlikely to assume that final certainty is possible and start pronouncing on the plays with an unjustified degree of assurance.

The present investigation into the nature of Shakespeare's inexhaustibility will, I hope, reflect a similar caution. At various points I shall work back from the plays themselves to what Shakespeare may have had consciously in mind when he started writing them. An assumption I shall make (it is hardly a radical or contentious one) is that not all the effects in each play were premeditated and worked out in advance – in other words, that Shakespeare's original intentions must in varying degrees have been expanded in the course of composition.[5]

Nevertheless, it is one thing to concede this much in general terms about the way that Shakespeare, like many other writers, may have worked. It is quite another to set out to identify the process in specific detail in particular plays. We do not have access to Shakespeare's mind and therefore cannot know what his dramatic intentions were, nor how much or how little they may eventually have been changed. Why then pursue these matters at all?

I have already suggested why it is permissible, even desirable, to take some note of a writer's intentions. In the case of Shakespeare the compelling reason for doing so is my belief – it is the central thread in everything that follows – that Shakespeare creates effects which are very much more complex, even contradictory, than the general structure of a particular play leads us to expect. In this connection there is an important distinction to be drawn between complexity and contradiction. Complexity implies a mutually sustaining balance of conflicting qualities; contradiction implies the absence or destruction of that balance. The distinction is between those aspects of a play which are mutually reinforcing and those which are mutually exclusive. Being made to feel, say, a fine balance of sympathy and condemnation for a tragic hero would indicate complexity. The sensation that at different points the play seemed to be urging us to adopt one attitude to the exclusion of the other would suggest contradiction. The relation of this distinction to questions of intention is that complexity is the expression of a coherent intention, or set of intentions, on the part of the dramatist. In a work which is complex but wholly integrated, discussion of Shakespeare's intentions is peculiarly difficult; they have dissolved into the work itself. Contradiction, on the other hand, logically implies the presence of two or more opposed impulses or intentions. The question of whether one impulse had priority in Shakespeare's mind can be resolved, conjecturally at best, by noting the extent to which it seems to have shaped the broad structure of the play.

It is not part of my purpose to impose a general schema on Shakespeare's work. The plays dealt with in the next three chapters exemplify different kinds of complexity and contradiction, and Shakespeare's initial intentions with each play, so far as they can be assessed at all, seem to have been correspondingly different. *Love's Labour's Lost* appears to have been, by Shakespeare's standards, relatively simple in its original conception; *Henry IV, Part 1* more complex; so also *Part 2* – though, as I shall argue later, its complexity is somewhat reduced by the end of the play. And *The Tempest* seems to me to hint at unresolved contradictory intentions.

Conjectures such as these, it cannot too often be stressed, remain finally unprovable, and the reason for taking discussion of Shakespeare into these speculative regions at all is that it may enable us to understand better the plays as they actually exist.

II

In interpreting Shakespeare what we bring to him is what we bring to all writers: ourselves – what we are, what we know, what we have read, what we feel, think and believe. One part of Shakespeare's pre-eminence lies in a greater capacity than other writers to draw more of our experience into play in responding to his work. It is hard to get our minds and imaginations all round Shakespeare, harder still to articulate everything we derive from the attempt. This fact helps to explain the existence of different identifiable critical approaches to Shakespeare; the particular aspects of our experience that we bring to bear determine the kind of approach we adopt. It should be added, of course, that critics do not write to a pattern and that any critic can be taken to exemplify more than one of the approaches listed below. They are offered as rough guides, intended primarily to provide a framework for the discussion of Shakespeare criticism in the next three chapters.

Contemporary meanings of Shakespeare's language. No one would dispute that it is necessary to know what the words mean. It can sometimes be necessary to know how they are pronounced as well. When in *As You Like it* Touchstone says, 'And so, from hour to hour, we ripe and ripe', we mistake a bawdy joke for mere philosophical banality if we fail to realise that there is a pun on 'hour' and 'whore' and that 'ripe' also means 'search'. Although it is as much a precondition of all other approaches as one in itself, this approach does not confine itself to editorial elucidation. Claudio's brief references to his relationship with Juliet in *Measure for Measure* have given rise to scholarly discussion of his precise marital status under Elizabethan law.

Topical meanings. Again, this may be just a matter of local elucidation, but in some cases this approach can involve treating a whole play as a *drame à clef*. Examples are F. A. Yates's *A Study of 'Love's Labour's Lost'* and M. C. Bradbrook's *The School of Night*, both of which seek to illuminate hidden satirical references to contemporary figures in *Love's Labour's Lost*. Less directly explicatory but possibly more well known is Leslie Hotson's *The First Night of 'Twelfth Night'*, an attempted reconstruction of what it was like to be present at the first performance of the play. Shakespeare's sonnets, naturally enough, have come in for much of this kind of treatment, and there are many studies which seek to explain them through establishing the identity of the unknown young man and the dark lady.

Source criticism. The plays can be approached by means of Shakespeare's source material – the prose romances and translations of Italian *novelle* for his comedies, the English chroniclers for the history plays. Even works by other dramatists are grist to Shakespeare's mill. In the transformation of *The True Chronicle History of King Leir* into *King Lear* the similarity of the characters' names and general plot combined with the dissimilarity of the plays' endings (King Leir gets his kingdom back and survives happily) indicate Shakespeare's use of and the extent of his departure from his source. J. A. K. Thomson's *Shakespeare and the Classics* and Carol Gesner's *Shakespeare and the Greek Romance* deal with Shakespeare's use of classical literature. Although there is no absolute distinction between source and influence, I have kept questions of general cultural influences on Shakespeare as a separate approach. The known sources for the plays are assembled in Geoffrey Bullough's eight-volume *Narrative and Dramatic Sources of Shakespeare*; a concise but comprehensive critical interpretation of them is contained in Kenneth Muir's *The Sources of Shakespeare's Plays*.

Contemporary dramatic conditions. Through understanding the nature of the Elizabethan theatre – the physical structure of the theatres, the dramatic effects they were capable of, the composition of the companies – we are able to see more clearly the external conditions which influenced the way Shakespeare wrote. This can give rise to such theories as that the reason Falstaff did not appear in *Henry V* is that Will Kemp had left the company; or that the Romances were the result of Shakespeare's company's acquiring the Blackfriars theatre, where he was now writing for a coterie audience. Less ambitious but probably more convincing explanations of how the external constraints of Shakespeare's theatre influenced how he wrote are contained in Nevill Coghill's *Shakespeare's Professional Skills* and J. L. Styan's *Shakespeare's Stagecraft*.

Contemporary dramatic conventions. This approach originated in the need to eliminate misunderstandings caused by interpreting Shakespeare's plays in terms appropriate to the drama of a later age, in particular by the naïve application of ideas derived from nineteenth-century natural-ism. A pioneer work of this kind was S. L. Bethell's *Shakespeare and the Popular Dramatic Tradition*. Such investigations were at first reductive, confining Shakespeare's art to the primitive dramatic techniques of his contemporaries and predecessors. More recent studies, however, have revealed the extent of Shakespeare's originality in transforming his inherited material – for example, Leo Salingar's *Shakespeare and the Traditions of Comedy*, Rosalie L. Colie's *Shakespeare's Living Art*, and Emrys Jones's *The Origins of Shakespeare*.

Contemporary beliefs. An understanding of the moral, religious or political beliefs of Shakespeare's age, obscured in part for later audiences, can throw light on the kind of assumptions Shakespeare would have made in writing his plays. Such studies often gravitate into debate about what Shakespeare himself believed; for instance, the claim, first put forward in E. M. W. Tillyard's *Shakespeare's History Plays*, that Shakespeare echoed the traditional Tudor doctrine on civil obedience, has since been much disputed, most recently by John Wilders in *The Lost Garden*. The general question of Shakespeare's relationship to his cultural environment is well examined in Wilbur Sanders's *The Dramatist and the Received Idea*.

Shakespeare and Christianity. Although this is strictly an aspect of the preceding approach, there has been enough written on the presence or absence of Christian thought in Shakespeare's plays to merit a separate category. An investigation of the plays' metaphysical assumptions forms the basis of W. R. Elton's *'King Lear' and the Gods* and H. A. Kelly's *Divine Providence in the England of Shakespeare's History Plays*. Peter Milward in *Shakespeare's Religious Background* has the dramatist harking back regretfully to the unity of pre-Reformation England. The belief that Shakespeare's religious views are both orthodox and discernible in the plays is asserted by R. W. Battenhouse in *Shakespearean Tragedy: Its Art and Its Christian Premises* and questioned by R. M. Frye in *Shakespeare and Christian Doctrine*.

Impressionistic or 'creative' criticism. A contrast to the sober endeavours of historical criticism, this attempts not to explain or evaluate but to re-create the essence of the work in question – criticism as a second-order creative act. Walter Pater's account of the *Mona Lisa*, which Yeats later cast into free verse, is the most notorious non-Shakespearean example of this kind of criticism. Although critics allow themselves the occasional purple passage, this form of criticism is never wholly self-sufficient, even in Pater's Shakespeare criticism. This did not stop T. S. Eliot from remarking on one occasion that we should be grateful Pater did not fix his attention on *Hamlet*.

Genre criticism. The decision by the editors of the First Folio to group the plays into comedies, histories and tragedies has encouraged critics to analyse the relations of plays within each group. There are innumerable such studies, as well as studies of sub-genres such as the 'problem play' or 'problem comedy'. Difficulties of definition, resulting from the attempt to elicit common features, occur not only within the sub-genres but within the major ones as well. Critics have started to find it at least as profitable to explore connections, between plays that cut across earlier notions of genre – for instance, between the Roman and history plays. It is a rash critic today who would attempt to advance a comprehensive theory of Shakespearean tragedy; in the words of Kenneth Muir, 'There is no such thing as Shakespearian Tragedy: there are only Shakespearian tragedies.'[6]

Character criticism. Probably the most popular of all forms of Shakespeare criticism, it has been under something of a cloud for much of this century. Its fall into disfavour was largely the result of a tendency by some critics to wander off into irrelevant biographical speculation, as if dramatic characters were the same as people in real life. Nevertheless, a work such as John Palmer's *Political and Comic Characters of Shakespeare* demonstrates how much this approach has to contribute to our understanding of Shakespeare. As an inevitable tribute to Shakespeare's insight into human nature, twentieth-century developments in psychology have been reflected in criticism of the plays. Undoubtedly the most well-known is Ernest Jones's discussion of *Hamlet*, which sees the Prince as the possessor of an unresolved Oedipus complex. The most comprehensive survey of Freudian interpretations of Shakespeare is contained in Norman Holland's *Psychoanalysis and Shakespeare*. More recently, A. Aronson in *Psyche and Symbol in Shakespeare* has argued for a Jungian interpretation of the plays, in which the dramatist's chief concern is with the individuation of the main characters.

Ritual, myth and archetype. This way of viewing Shakespeare owes something to Jung and possibly rather more to James Frazer's *The Golden Bough*. A work acknowledging a direct debt to Jung is Maud Bodkin's *Archetypal Patterns in Poetry*, which has some discussion of *Hamlet, King Lear* and *Othello*. Shakespeare's particularity of treatment makes his plays resistant to the eliciting of archetypal or mythic patterns; at all events, this approach has not produced a substantial body of criticism. It figures in Northrop Frye's *Anatomy of Criticism* and colours his subsequent books on Shakespeare's comedies and tragedies, *A Natural Perspective* and *The Fools of Time*. John Holloway in *The Story of the Night* makes much of the scapegoat motif in the tragedies. This whole approach to Shakespeare is given a thorough, albeit sceptical, consideration in an appendix, 'Myth, Symbol, and Poetry', to Hallett Smith's *Shakespeare's Romances*.

Analysis of imagery and metaphor. This approach can probably claim to be the twentieth century's most significant contribution to our understanding of Shakespeare. In the 1930s his plays came to be seen less as poetic dramas than as dramatic poems. The approach was pioneered by G. Wilson Knight, who in his first book, *The Wheel of Fire*, suggested that we should respond to Shakespeare in spatial rather than temporal terms and see the plays as expanded metaphors. The possibility that the poetry might give us direct access to Shakespeare's mind was investigated by Caroline Spurgeon in *Shakespeare's Imagery and What It Tells Us*, and, with a greater literary sensitivity, by E. A. Armstrong in *Shakespeare's Imagination*. The metaphoric structure of some of the plays and their reliance on a single controlling metaphor are the subject of R. B. Heilman's *This Great Stage: Image and Structure in 'King Lear'* and Ralph Berry's *The Shakespearean Metaphor*.

Themes. The use of the term itself is fairly recent, but the idea behind it is implicit in any attempt to say what the plays are about. It is there, for instance, in the moral which Dr Johnson sought to draw from the plays – the attempt sometimes accompanied by a rebuke for Shakespeare's failure to make it sufficiently obvious. Thematic criticism tends in varying degrees to be moralistic in tone, and there are inevitable problems about trying to sum up the significance of a writer as complex as Shakespeare in a convenient phrase. John Holloway in *The Story of the Night* claims that this kind of criticism, represented chiefly, in his view, by Wilson Knight, L. C. Knights and Derek Traversi, results in the reduction of the power and complexity of a Shakespeare play to a handful of moralisms which are at best banal and at worst absurd.

Shakespeare as man and thinker. Using the plays to draw conclusions about Shakespeare's mind and personality, or at least his opinions, derives from the Romantic assumption that a writer expresses his personality in his work. An influential nineteenth-century study was Edward Dowden's *Shakspere: A Critical Study of His Mind and Art*. In the present century this approach has been taken up by critics as varied as Caroline Spurgeon in *Shakespeare's Imagery* and L. C. Knights in *Some Shakespearean Themes*. A connection between this approach and the preceding one is that, for Knights, the themes of the plays are an articulation of deeply felt concerns of Shakespeare himself.

Theatrical criticism. Once somewhat neglected, this is now increasingly recognised as an important dimension to the study of the plays. The classic work is Harley Granville-Barker's *Prefaces to Shakespeare*. John Russell Brown has furthered this approach in *Shakespeare's Plays in Performance*, while Marvin Rosenberg gives a theatrical criticism in *The Masks of Othello* and *The Masks of King Lear*, and Arnold Goldman bases his *Shakespeare and the Energies of Drama* on an awareness of what happens on stage. Stanley Wells in *Royal Shakespeare* and Richard David in *Shakespeare in the Theatre* combine a study of particular productions with analyses of the plays themselves. The growing influence of the theatre on academics and their influence in turn on directors are reviewed by J. L. Styan in *The Shakespeare Revolution*.

Structural criticism. Although most critics are concerned in varying degrees with the structure of the plays, this aspect of Shakespeare has received most concentrated and specialised attention from a number of American critics. R. S. Crane has a chapter on 'Monistic Criticism and the Structure of Shakespearean Drama' in *The Languages of Criticism and the Structure of Poetry*, and Francis Fergusson wrote on '*Macbeth* as the Imitation of an Action' in *English Institute Essays 1951*. Fergusson's *The Idea of a Theater* also has chapters on Shakespeare. These works draw on ideas from Aristotle's *Poetics*, as does a more recent study, A. L. Birney's *Satiric Catharsis in Shakespeare: A Theory of Dramatic Structure*.

Shakespeare the self-conscious questioner of his art. This approach sees Shakespeare's plays as concerned with, and even conducting an investigation into, the nature and value of his art. His artistic self-awareness is the subject of Anne Righter's *Shakespeare and the Idea of the Play*; it forms part of Nigel Alexander's study of *Hamlet* in *Poison Play and Duel*; and it underlies Robert Egan's *Drama Within Drama: Shakespeare's Sense of his Art in 'King Lear', 'The Winter's Tale' and 'The Tempest'*. Shakespeare's simultaneous belief in and scepticism about his shapings of reality are considered by Philip Edwards in *Shakespeare and the Confines of Art*. The approach has been taken to its furthest extreme in J. L. Calderwood's *Shakespearean Metadrama*, which treats the plays as self-referring works of art about art.

Marxist criticism. Shakespeare is a far from easy subject for this approach, both because his plays have little of a dogmatic spirit about them and because they offer less direct observation and re-creation of Shakespeare's society than plays by many of his contemporaries. Brecht's Berliner Ensemble production of *Coriolanus* required a considerable revision of the text in order to make its point about the class war. Russian Shakespeare criticism has produced most examples of this approach; A. A. Smirnov's *Shakespeare: A Marxist Interpretation* was translated in 1936. More finely responsive accounts of the plays are contained in *Shakespeare and Society* by Terence Eagleton and *Shakespeare in a Changing World*, edited by Arnold Kettle.

Twentieth-century interpretations. The view of Shakespeare as making art the subject of his art, mentioned above, seems to draw some of its inspiration from parallel tendencies in modern poetry. G. K. Hunter in *Dramatic Identities and Cultural Tradition* is enlightening about the effect of the symbolist aesthetic on the Shakespeare criticism of T. S. Eliot and Wilson Knight. But probably the most well-known example of this kind of criticism is Jan Kott's *Shakespeare Our Contemporary*, which, though not wholly anti-historical in bias, is most memorable for its references to concentration camps, the police state and the atomic bomb.

III

This sketch of the different ways in which Shakespeare has been approached and discussed gives some idea of the remarkable diversity of response to the plays. The source of this diversity is, as I have indicated, the underlying concern of the rest of the book. Subsequent chapters are not only studies of individual plays; they are also studies of some of the critics who have written on them and of the critical approaches which they exemplify. I do not propose to deal explicitly with all the approaches summarised above, but the discussion of the major ones will, I hope, provide a frame of reference for the reader who is so minded to make his own assessment of those not considered in detail. Through seeing where critics are helpful or unhelpful, which approaches are most useful, the ways in which an approach can be skilfully or clumsily employed, I hope to establish a conception of Shakespeare's artistry that will explain how all these wide-ranging and conflicting interpretations have arisen.

At this point the sceptical reader will wonder what such theorising about Shakespeare can possibly be worth. It will be – it is bound to be – simply one person's opinion: at best, just one more interpretation.

We are back peering into the abyss of relativism, and I had better repeat why we both can and should refrain from plunging over the edge. There are two main reasons. The theoretical one is the argument presented in the earlier part of this chapter: any work of literature (including a Shakespeare play) has a limitedly objective existence conferred upon it by the very stuff of which it is composed – the words the writer has used. Because, to an extent, it objectively exists, then to that extent it is objectively discussable. As a result literary criticism is, within these necessary but ill-defined limits, a rational activity in which appeals to the evidence can legitimately be made to defend or refute a particular interpretation – such as the view of Shakespeare that will emerge during the course of this book.

My second reason not only for rejecting relativism but also for claiming objective authority for the views on Shakespeare that follow is one that, I must admit, is far from logically watertight, but I hope it will have a pragmatic cogency. It is that they are as much traditional as original, and I intend later on to show them growing naturally out of what I take to be the central tradition of Shakespeare criticism. The case I am arguing should look less strange when finally set in the context of this tradition. In short, the authority for my views will derive from the number of others they resemble and the extent to which in the end they seem familiar.

2 *Love's Labour's Lost*

The attempt to see what is distinctively Shakespearean about Shakespeare requires a consideration of plays at both ends of his dramatic career; for that reason a later chapter will be devoted to *The Tempest*. *Love's Labour's Lost*, however, is a useful play with which to begin, for, besides being an early work, it has the further advantage of being a comparatively simple one. Despite the many studies of Shakespearean comedy in the last twenty-five years, there has been little disagreement about what constitutes its basic outline. This is hardly surprising. It would be difficult to produce a radical reinterpretation of the play without wilful eccentricity. In the words of a recent critic, 'The central action of *Labor's* is, roughly speaking, the adjustment by Navarre's academy to the claims of flesh and blood.'[1] The play is a satirical presentation of various kinds of affectation and artifice, setting them against an awareness of the normality and reality from which they depart. Shorn of the evidences of imperfect revision and the occasional passage of impenetrable obscurity, it develops in an unbroken line to its conclusion. The fact that it is a satire (not a dramatic mode to which elsewhere Shakespeare seems much attracted) means that it announces its significance with a near-explicitness that is rare in his work. The play is neat, pointed, tending even to the diagrammatic, a construction of interlocking parts; some at least of its appeal is to the pleasure we take in formal perfection.

That must seem a singularly bloodless way of putting it. But I am emphasising for the moment this play's resistance to the contradictoriness evident in the criticism of many of Shakespeare's other works. If we can broadly agree on what *Love's Labour's Lost* essentially is, it becomes that much easier to agree on what it is not. It is a good play in which to demonstrate erroneous and unhelpful views and approaches. With not many of Shakespeare's plays can we start with a broad consensus of critical opinion. With this one we can.

Having said that, I want immediately to qualify the impression of *Love's Labour's Lost* as a limited, finite, and ultimately perhaps rather simple-minded work. It contains elements which create a greater richness and depth than the preceding comments would suggest, but they also render it less than perfectly articulated, less than wholly consistent. Shakespeare has almost put more into this play than it will hold, so that there is a tension, increasingly noticeable as the action proceeds, between its form and its content. The sacrifice of formal perfection is the price that is paid for the play's experiential fullness. And it is the price that is paid in many if not most of Shakespeare's plays.

I

In order to substantiate that last claim I want to start with a general point which applies not only to *Love's Labour's Lost* but to all the plays. It is of the importance of attending to everything that they contain: as far as possible we should avoid basing our interpretations on a consciously or unconsciously selective reading. I imagine this injunction is sufficiently uncontentious, not to say trite, for it not to need much stress. The fact remains that it has not always been observed in practice – or even in theory.

For a long time *Love's Labour's Lost* was one of the most neglected and disparaged of Shakespeare's comedies, earning the special distinction from Hazlitt of being the one play by Shakespeare we could possibly do without. But in this century the play was rediscovered, and it became clear that in the theatre it worked extremely well. Much of the credit for this must go to Harley Granville-Barker, whose *Prefaces to Shakespeare* are still well worth consulting. But for all his sense of *Love's Labour's Lost*'s theatrical potential, his critical comments on the play are such as to make him a most uncertain guide. For him the play works well by virtue of one quality, its style:

> If the music is clear and fine, as Elizabethan music was, if the costumes strike their note of fantastic beauty, if, above all, the speech and movements of the actors are fine and rhythmical too, then this quaint medley of mask and play can still be made delightful. But it asks for style in the acting. The whole play, first and last, demands style. . . . We must have a beauty of speech that will leave us a little indifferent to the sense of the thing spoken. Navarre and his friends

and their ladies must show such distinction and grace that we ask no
more pleasure in their company.[2]

The play demands style because the subject matter is so thin. Granville-
Barker regards it as largely a comedy of verbal affectations belonging
too much to Shakespeare's own day to be of real interest to us. The
elegant posturings and wit belong to characters who fail to come alive
for us, and from this general lack of human interest we must salvage
what we can by concentrating on manner rather than matter. Berowne,
it is acknowledged, presents a realistic perspective on this world of
shams and affectations from a position slightly outside it. So too do the
Princess and her ladies; but they 'are not, and cannot be made, much
more than mouthpieces for wit and good sense'.[3] The unifying gloss over
the patchy but generally thin surface of this work is summed up in the
word 'style'.

There are any number of quibbles one might make about this
account. It is not true that the affectations are exclusively verbal, nor do
they belong exclusively to Shakespeare's time. Equally it is untrue (I
shall argue this later) that the relations between the courtiers and their
ladies are restricted to the surface sparkle of the combats of wit. The
source of these misreadings lies essentially in the critic's own recommendation to be a little indifferent to the sense of the thing spoken. It forms
an open invitation to miss those aspects of the play which a greater
attentiveness might have revealed. It will almost certainly result, as
here, in a deficient reading of the play.

Paradoxically, an inattentive response can not only make *Love's
Labour's Lost* seem less substantial than it in fact is, it can also ascribe to
the play philosophical depths that are not there. In Act IV scene iii
Berowne delivers a long, magnificent speech asserting the claims of love
over those of study. In it he draws on a stock of neo-Platonic ideas which
were expressed by many of Shakespeare's contemporaries with total
seriousness. As a result the speech has similarly been regarded as
belonging in a quite straightforward way to that tradition:

> Berowne is but the mouthpiece of them all. He and they have learned
> the difference between sensual love and love of woman for her mind
> and soul. He is well advanced toward the Italian ideal of rational
> love, and a woman's eyes have been his book.[4]

We are certainly not in the sphere of ordinary love-making; if this is not nonsense, it must be philosophy; and there is a Marsilian ring in the concluding lines:

> Let us once lose our oaths to find ourselves,
> Or else we lose ourselves to keep our oaths.
> It is religion to be thus forsworn,
> For charity itself fulfils the law,
> And who can sever love from charity?   (iv iii 357–61)

As in Ficino, the climax of the ascent is the finding of the true self in deity.[5]

Now Berowne clearly vindicates the right of love to exert sovereignty over study:

> For when would you my liege, or you, or you,
> In leaden contemplation have found out
> Such fiery numbers as the prompting eyes
> Of beauty's tutors have enriched you with?
>   (ll. 316–19)

It is a fine and profound speech. Beauty is the only origin of understanding, the true impulsive force behind all learning.[6]

These critics (the first two especially) illustrate the misuse of that historical approach which employs an awareness of contemporary ideas and beliefs to illuminate the plays. All three overlook the element of irony in Berowne's references to the Platonic tradition and consequently treat them with an inappropriate solemnity, finding profundity of thought where none was intended.

We should be less likely to deceive ourselves about the speech, even if we look at it from the point of view of sixteenth-century neo-Platonism, if we remember that truth is the last thing that the King, Dumain and Longaville want. What they want is 'some flattery for this evil. . . . Some salve for perjury' (ll. 282, 285). They want to get round the fact of their broken oaths, and all they require from Berowne is a tissue of rhetoric sufficiently plausible to still their consciences and let them get on with wooing the ladies of France.

In these circumstances Berowne's speech was bound to rest on fraudulent logic. It is a whirling combination of truths, half-truths and untruths, and the quality of the poetry is a remarkably sensitive indicator of how true or specious is that which is being expressed. It is no accident that the most often quoted lines are:

> It adds a precious seeing to the eye:
> A lover's eyes will gaze an eagle blind.
> A lover's ears will hear the lowest sound,
> When the suspicious head of theft is stopp'd.
> Love's feeling is more soft and sensible
> Than are the tender horns of cockled snails.
>
> (ll. 329–34)

But Berowne has to 'prove' that love does more than quicken the senses. Yet everything else he says carries increasingly less conviction (because it is less true), and the poetry is consequently inferior, with its rhetorical questions ('is not Love a Hercules . . . ?' – l. 336) and classical references piled up in order to reinforce the argument. The speech reaches a climax in two lines where obscurity of meaning makes it impossible to elicit more than a vague sense of unfocused emotion: 'And when Love speaks, the voice of all the gods/Make heaven drowsy with the harmony' (ll. 340–1). From obscurity Berowne passes on to what is clear, and yet clearly untrue:

> Never durst poet touch a pen to write
> Until his ink were temp'red with Love's sighs;
> O, then his lines would ravish savage ears,
> And plant in tyrants mild humility.   (ll. 342–5)

And with that he is off on his final peroration. But it is entirely fitting that the last three lines should be the inverted major and minor premises and conclusion of a syllogistic argument – and that the argument should be invalid:

> It is religion to be thus forsworn;
> For charity itself fulfils the law,
> And who can sever love from charity?   (ll. 359–61)

II

Even if the two preceding approaches to *Love's Labour's Lost* have not proved very productive, the fact that the critics concerned had a discernible approach at least gave clarity and shape to what each had to say. It was an organised response, not a mere jumble of unrelated perceptions. Without some organising principle response remains inchoate and unformed. The reason why early commentators on this play such as Johnson, Coleridge and Hazlitt are so unhelpful is not merely that it did not engage them very deeply, it is that they failed to synthesise what impressions the play made.

There is, it must be admitted, a problem about the term 'approach'. Almost by definition it implies something limiting and restrictive. If a critic is identifiable as using one approach, he has presumably omitted or excluded everything that may be revealed through other approaches. 'Approach' even has a faintly opprobrious ring to it; other people have their own (necessarily limited) approach to Shakespeare's plays; you and I respond to the plays with a more comprehensive fullness. On the other hand, if there is nothing in the way someone writes or talks about Shakespeare that is not to some degree identifiable as his particular approach, the chances are that he is taking us on a directionless meander through the play in question. What we are entitled to ask of a critic is that he supplies an interpretation, not a scattering of impressions. And an interpretation cannot be arrived at without something round which it is organised, something which gives it stability and coherence. No one (not even a critic) likes to be pigeon-holed. But on balance it may be better to settle for being pigeon-holed than be accused of incoherence or vacuousness.

The problem for the critic is to achieve clarity and definition without omissions, false over-simplifications, or exaggerated one-sidedness. Of course, it cannot be done. All anyone can hope is to avoid the grosser forms of these errors.

Edward Dowden was the first nineteenth-century critic to produce a clearly argued interpretation of *Love's Labour's Lost*; it had a certain solidity; it offered useful resistance to the reader trying to define his own reactions to the play. Part of its value stemmed from the fact that Dowden knew what he was looking for in Shakespeare. He was attempting to lay bare Shakespeare's soul and to investigate the plays for the light they threw on the dramatist's spiritual and intellectual development:

[*Love's Labour's Lost*] is a satirical extravaganza embodying Shakespeare's criticism upon contemporary fashions and foibles of speech, in manners and literature. . . . It is a protest against youthful schemes of shaping life according to notions rather than according to reality, a protest against idealizing away the facts of life. The play is chiefly interesting as containing Shakespeare's confession of faith with respect to the true principles of self-culture. . . . Here, he says, we are with such and such appetites and passions. Let us in any scheme of self-development get *that* fact acknowledged at all events. Otherwise, we shall quickly enough betray ourselves as arrant fools, fit to be flouted by women, and needing to learn from them a portion of their directness, practicality, and good sense.[7]

Although as criticism this is a distinct improvement on Dowden's predecessors, its virtues simultaneously define its limitations. Dowden's biographical concern with Shakespeare's alleged inner development probably led him to derive a nourishment from *Love's Labour's Lost* that was not there, not at least in the form in which he described it. Is it true, for instance, that 'The play is *chiefly* interesting as containing Shakespeare's confession of faith with respect to the true principles of self-culture'? – even if we grant that the principles are there in the first place.

By contrast, H. B. Charlton is clear what he is looking for in the play and is equally clear that it is not present. For him a play must have a convincing plot and plausible characterisation, and in both respects *Love's Labour's Lost* is sadly deficient:

But the worst consequences of the poverty of the story appear in the persons who perform in it. The four courtiers could not but resemble each other in a wooden conformity; for they all have to do the same sort of thing, and have all to be guilty of an act of almost incredible stupidity. To have attempted human differentiation would have been to explore a world of the spirit where deep-rooted passions, conflicting instincts, and complex promptings mould distinctive personalities; and thereby to have made the oath-taking impossible. Hence the courtiers in the play lack personality, and are equally without typical character of the human sort.[8]

Heavy criticism indeed – not to say heavy-handed. Charlton's concern about Shakespeare's failure to create believable and adequately motivated characters makes him ironically rebuke Navarre for being 'a king who runs away from public life on a harebrain scheme without even so much foresight as to appoint a deputy who might inform enquirers that his present address is unknown'.[9] This surely takes an over-literal view of Navarre's kingdom and of his responsibilities to it. The political background to the play is sketched in by Shakespeare with such amiable lack of precision that obviously it is not there that our attention is meant to be directed. Does anyone, after all, remotely understand either in the theatre or even on successive rereadings Navarre's speech (II i 128–52) in which he purports to explain the quarrel between himself and the King of France?

An over-exclusive concentration on character can blind one to other aspects of the play. M. M. Mahood's approach is through the play's linguistic qualities:

> Love's Labour's Lost is the first play in which Shakespeare boldly questions the truth of words. A repeated quibble upon light points to the play's central theme that words, for all their witty sparkle, are without weight or substance. . . . The facts of nature prove stronger than verbal resolves, and the courtiers are forced to explain away their perjury (a keyword of the play) with 'vowes are but breath, and breath a vapour is'. . . . The Princess and her companions, for all the brilliance of their wordplay, are sceptical of words from the start. To prove afresh the frailty of speech they trick their lovers into breaking a new set of vows, those of constancy . . . and Berowne is despatched to discover the hollowness of words by jesting in a hospital.[10]

Although Professor Mahood's 'central theme' is certainly there in the play, its centrality is questionable. The play is about the insubstantial nature of words as part of a more comprehensive theme: the hollowness and insubstantiality of certain attitudes and behaviour. The result of trying to give too great an emphasis to this single aspect of the play is inevitably a slight forcing of the evidence. The trick played by the ladies on their lovers proves nothing whatever about the frailties of speech; it merely illustrates the fact that if you deliberately set out to deceive someone, you frequently can succeed. And Berowne is not despatched to a hospital to discover the hollowness of words; he is sent there to discover whether they are hollow or not.

III

The critics just looked at reflect what is probably the commonest fault of

Shakespeare criticism: the underlying argument has been over-extended, and what is peripheral or at least secondary is offered as central and crucial. For a critical argument to be stigmatised as off-centre there presumably has to be a sense of what by contrast is more genuinely central. The difficulty with many Shakespeare plays is that opinion is divided on what can be regarded as the central core. But *Love's Labour's Lost*, as I said earlier, is a relatively simple work, and I want now to summarise two accounts of it which in broad outline and many of the details would, I imagine, command a large measure of assent.

E. M. W. Tillyard sees the play as having two main strands, 'The mocking of the male adolescence' and 'The feast of words'. Navarre and his companions are young, foolish and immature, and the play is a record both of their attempt to frame society according to immature ideals, and of how, in the process, the claims of a more rational ordering of society make themselves felt. The immaturity of the men is reflected, first, in their proposal for an Academe, to which they dedicate themselves with the idealism and self-ignorance of youth, and, secondly, when the Academe has collapsed, in their manner of wooing the ladies of France. Their wooing is in accordance with the theory of love that Berowne expounds, but shows no awareness of what the ladies they are supposed to be courting would themselves desire. The masque of the Muscovites is a fiasco, but even this does not lead the men to act with more discretion and self-awareness. The pageant of the Nine Worthies, coming after the humiliating conclusion of the courtiers' masque, provides them with an excuse for behaviour that attains a new degree of crudity. The arrival of Marcade ends the pageant and forces the various characters to take stock of the situation. When the men assert the genuineness of their love, the women decide to give them a chance to prove its real quality. The penances which they impose reinforce one theme of the play, which ridicules the callowness of youth and measures it by the requirements of social living.

The connection between this theme and 'The feast of words' is that adolescence is the time of life when men are most intoxicated by words, and it is appropriate to combine a gentle satire on spiritual immaturity with one on rhetorical excess. Much of the metrical experimentation in the play is, of course, Shakespeare's own; for instance, his use of iambic trimeters, rime royal, doggerel, quatrains, and so forth; but he also uses the opportunity afforded by Holofernes' epitaph on the deer to satirise the metrical forms that were then starting to go out of fashion.

Shakespeare's satire on language expresses itself mainly through Holofernes and Armado. In their polysyllabic extravagances Shakespeare holds up to ridicule linguistic affectation, pomposity and perversity. But the play's mocking spirit extends itself to the other characters as well. Part of Boyet's opening speech in Act II scene i, Tillyard suggests, is an echo of the rhetorical over-inflation of Armado's letter to the King in the first scene. And Berowne himself renounces 'Taffeta phrases, silken terms precise' (v ii 406) in a gesture that indulges what he is rejecting. 'Sans "sans", I pray you', reminds Rosaline (l. 416). The significance of the play, according to Tillyard, is that,

> It belongs, as I have said, to the central area of social comedy. Four young men, refusing to see things as they are, attempt a feat which common sense could have told them was impossible. That impossibility becomes quickly apparent, but even then they persist in their childish vision of reality. But society, in the form of four clear-sighted young women, and the unexpected irruption of the reality of death give them a series of lessons and put them on the way to seeing things as they are. Matching the four young men in their distorted vision of reality are two older men and the hanger-on of one of them. One of these distorts reality by clothing his spiritual nakedness in fantasies, and they both violate reality by enlarging the distance of words from the things they represent. They are fully grown and set in their habits and, unlike the young men, who are still malleable, they will continue to be comparatively harmless misfits in the society to which they belong. . . . Whatever becomes of the young men, they have, by the end of the play, quitted the old enclosure. In contrast, Armado and Holofernes will inhabit it for ever.[11]

In his study of *Love's Labour's Lost* Tillyard acknowledged a debt to an earlier essay by Anne Barton. The two accounts do not disagree on essentials but rather on where the main emphases come. For Dr Barton the play is, at its deepest level, about life and death and about ways of coming to terms with both. The two alternative ways of defeating 'cormorant devouring Time' (I i 4) and achieving immortality are those of fame and union in marriage. The vow taken at the beginning of the play is an expression of the Renaissance desire to find a permanence through devotion to learning. But the Academe itself is composed of different levels of artifice and reality. Besides artificial and virtually indistinguishable figures such as Dumain and Longaville, there is

Berowne, whose realistic insight penetrates the shams of the Academe even as he enters it. Equally realistic in a different way is Dull, who is totally incapable of striking artificial poses of any kind. Costard and Dull serve to keep the play in touch with a more familiar and real world, as well as to indicate the ultimate victory of reality over artifice and illusion. Armado, too, exists in a world of his own imagination, peopled by the heroes of antiquity, but neither are these strong enough to withstand the pressure of reality. The entire world of the play must eventually be destroyed by forces from outside its walls.

The forces are those of life and death. The play opens with Navarre's reference to death in the first speech. The ladies, the intruders from the outside world, bring death into the park when the Princess kills a deer. In the last act we are reminded of Katharine's sister who died of melancholy, and through this anecdote love is linked in the ladies' minds with death, thus making the courtiers' love seem a mere pose. With the darkening of the atmosphere at the end of the play we are offered images of death ('Judas was hanged on an elder', 'A death's face in a ring', 'The sweet war-man is dead and rotten' – v ii 599, 605, 652), all of which serve as a prelude for the entrance of Marcade with his news of the death of the Princess's father. By contrast the ladies themselves represent the positive forces of life:

> The Princess and her little retinue represent the first penetration of the park by the normal world beyond, a world composed of different and colder elements than the fairy-tale environment within. Through them, in some sense, the voice of Reality speaks, and although they seem to fit perfectly into the landscape of the park, indulge in highly formal, elaborate skirmishes of wit with each other and with the men, they are somehow detached from this world of illusion and artificiality in a way that none of its original inhabitants are. . . . With them into the park they bring past time and a disturbing reminder of the world outside, and from them come the first objective criticisms which pass beyond the scheme of the Academe to attack the men who have formed it.[12]

By the fourth act the courtiers are in love, and the Academe has collapsed. At this stage Shakespeare introduces, in the persons of Holofernes and Nathaniel, 'reminders of what such a scheme might have led to, examples of the sterility of learning that is unrelated to life'. In this scene Dull represents once again the realistic element, 'the voice of the cuckoo which mocks, unconsciously, the intricate speech of the pedants'.[13] But fortunately for the courtiers the real world exerts an increasing influence, a process culminating in the penances which the ladies impose on their suitors at the end of the play as a test of the strength and reality of their love.

> It was this reality of actual living that Berowne was unconscious of when he led the unthinking merriment of the play scene just past. Yet, at the end of the year, love's labors will be won for Berowne, and he will receive Rosaline's love, not in the half real world of the park, but in the actuality outside its walls. Thus the play which began with a paradox, that of the Academe, closes with one as well. Only through the acceptance of the reality of Death are life and love in their fullest sense possible for the people of the play.[14]

These two accounts of *Love's Labour's Lost* indicate much of the richness and subtlety of what most people would agree to be the central movement of the play: the gradual confrontation of a world characterised by artifice with all that that world excludes. The process is a remorseless one, and the chill that follows first Marcade's entrance and then the final penalties imposed on the now sober courtiers is not felt by them alone. It is of a piece with this changed atmosphere that *Love's Labour's Lost* is the only one of Shakespeare's comedies not to end in marriage. The untraditional nature of the ending is emphasised by Berowne in words the effect of which is partially to dissolve the fabric of the play-world itself:

> BEROWNE   Our wooing doth not end like an old play:
> Jack hath not Jill. These ladies' courtesy
> Might well have made our sport a comedy.
> KING   Come, sir, it wants a twelvemonth an' a day,
> And then 'twill end.
> BEROWNE   That's too long for a play.
>
> (v ii 862–6)

All that the courtiers, and we, are left with are the songs of spring and winter, the springtime note of the cuckoo mocking married men, and the merry call of the owl in winter indifferent to the frozen rustics. The world outside the Academe beckons, and part of its chilly reality is that it remains an open question whether the courtiers can look forward with confidence to their delayed marriages twelve months hence; in the ladies' final words to their respective suitors, the Princess and Rosaline offer only conditional acceptance, while Katharine and Maria are merely pert.

The enlarging vistas at the conclusion of *Love's Labour's Lost* give it an open-ended quality, which in turn is an oblique testament to the fullness of experience that the play provides. At the beginning of this discussion I said that it seems superficially to be a limited work, its structure tending to the diagrammatic, its significance perhaps too easily accessible. The inadequacy of this view is illustrated not only by the play's ending but also by the way that, at points throughout its length, alternative possibilities of development suggest themselves to Shakespeare's imagination, possibilities which exemplify his generous inclusiveness but which involve a partial sacrifice of dramatic coherence and consistency.

IV

That is putting it generally. The accounts of Tillyard and Dr Barton share certain basic views about *Love's Labour's Lost*: that it is a romantic comedy with the conventional happy ending deferred; that the cause of the delay lies in the emotional immaturity of the men; and that the women's greater maturity (which is always emphasised elsewhere in Shakespeare's comedies) justifies them in imposing it.[15] This broad conception of the play is partially undermined by what was actually written; there is evidence of a different *kind* of play intermittently stimulating Shakespeare's imagination.

The difference is most apparent in the case of Berowne and Rosaline. Although he loves her, it seems that he has still to deserve her love in return even at the end of the play. Their relationship would appear to be defined by her courteous, dignified speech to him when he protests at his sentence to 'jest a twelvemonth in a hospital':

> Why, that's the way to choke a gibing spirit,
> Whose influence is begot of that loose grace
> Which shallow laughing hearers give to fools.
> A jest's prosperity lies in the ear
> Of him that hears it, never in the tongue
> Of him that makes it; then, if sickly ears,

> Deaf'd with the clamour of their own dear groans,
> Will hear your idle scorns, continue then,
> And I will have you and that fault withal.
> But if they will not, throw away that spirit,
> And I shall find you empty of that fault,
> Right joyful of your reformation.   (v ii 846–57)

It is a fine speech, determining the impression of both Rosaline and Berowne for us at the end, as Shakespeare no doubt intended that it should. But the earlier part of the play had from time to time revealed a somewhat different Rosaline and Berowne forming as a result a different relationship.

Berowne is obsessed with 'perjury'. It resonates throughout the play, and Berowne's obsession with it points to a deeper concern about his own integrity, violated twice: by breaking the solemn oath he had taken when he entered the Academe, and by breaking it for a girl whom – amazingly – he seems at times to despise. It is this dark undertow to Berowne's love for Rosaline that fleetingly alters the nature and balance of the entire play. There is an extra bitterness for him that it is for *this* woman he has broken his oath. The extent to which he feels dishonoured by his love for Rosaline is made clear in the soliloquy at the end of Act III scene i where he finally admits he is in love. The dominant tone, it is true, is of wryly comic exasperation. But in the final part of the speech Berowne returns, with what sounds like real bitterness, to the shame which he feels:

> Nay, to be perjur'd, which is worst of all;
> And, among three, to love the worst of all.
> A whitely wanton with a velvet brow,
> With two pitch balls stuck in her face for eyes;
> Ay, and, by heaven, one that will do the deed,
> Though Argus were her eunuch and her guard.
>
> (III i 184–9)

It would be difficult indeed to find a parallel for this in anything that Shakespeare's other romantic comedy heroes say about their ladies. The bile, self-disgust, and final eyebrow-raising accusation of Rosaline's promiscuity make this part of the speech only too reminiscent of Shakespeare's dark-lady sonnets; the physical description of Rosaline here and elsewhere in the play supplies a further parallel.

It would be inappropriate, however, for the speech to end on this
note, and Shakespeare's dramatic sense leads him to modulate from this
into the more relaxed note of the next six lines which conclude the scene:

> And I to sigh for her! to watch for her!
> To pray for her! Go to; it is a plague
> That Cupid will impose for my neglect
> Of his almighty dreadful little might.
> Well, I will love, write, sigh, pray, sue, and groan:
> Some men must love my lady, and some Joan.
>
> (ll. 190–5)

But when he next appears, at the beginning of Act ɪᴠ scene iii, the tone
of his opening soliloquy is far from the elegant posturings of the
conventional lover promised at the end of his last soliloquy:

> The King he is hunting the deer: I am coursing myself. They have
> pitch'd a toil: I am toiling in a pitch – pitch that defiles. Defile! a foul
> word. (ɪᴠ iii 1–3)

Yet even this speech follows a similar pattern to the one just described.
Here again he moves from momentary turmoil to an acceptance of what
he is, or, perhaps more accurately, the role he must play; and the end of
the speech with its note of more or less cheerful resignation ushers in the
richly comic scene in which the King, Dumain and Longaville are
shown to be in love also. This is the last time that these disturbing
undercurrents rise to trouble the surface of Berowne's love for Rosaline.
They do not occur often, and Shakespeare has not tried to integrate
them consistently into Berowne's character. What is curious is not that
they do not recur later but that they are there at all.

At all events their presence is no accident. For whatever reason – and
at whatever cost in terms of consistency – Shakespeare seems to have
wanted to evoke the degrading aspect of love as part of his treatment of
it in this play. A sense of how fatally Berowne has compromised his self-
respect, not only by breaking a solemn oath but by breaking it in the
service of a love which dishonours him, receives confirmation from an
unexpected quarter. Armado has sworn to study three years with the
other courtiers; and like them he has fallen in love:

> I do affect the very ground, which is base, where her shoe, which is

baser, guided by her foot, which is basest, doth tread. I shall be forsworn – which is a great argument of falsehood – if I love. And how can that be true love which is falsely attempted? Love is a familiar; Love is a devil. There is no evil angel but Love.   (I ii 158–63)

In saying, 'How can that be true love which is falsely attempted?', Armado is asking the same question as Berowne, the same one that the ladies put to the men at the end of the play. But, whereas Berowne has some insight into the quality of Rosaline, Armado seems to have very little into Jaquenetta, of whose promiscuity we are left in no doubt through Moth's jeering asides. Armado's courtship of a country girl who, like Rosaline, will 'do the deed', forms an ironic counterpoint to the wooing games indulged in by the courtiers. The parallel is maintained throughout the play, and at the very end Armado, besides accepting Jaquenetta's baby as his (though Costard, bringing the news, is no disinterested witness), accepts a penance like the other lords: 'I am a votary: I have vow'd to Jaquenetta to hold the plough for her sweet love three year.' (v ii 870–2).

There is no need to press too hard the parallel between Armado and Jaquenetta and the lords and their ladies. Shakespeare is not writing a first draft of *Troilus and Cressida*. Nevertheless, in his presentation of the ladies he seems to be pursuing two contradictory aims. He does indeed want to show them as embodying a greater maturity, self-possession and judgement than the young men. For at the end it is not enough that we acknowledge a basic justice in the courtiers' being despatched to hermitage and hospital to test the constancy of their love and to discover what life is really like. We must also be convinced that the ladies have the moral right to send them there; and for this purpose they must be seen to be slightly detached from – and superior to – the courtiers and their puppy-dog antics. But at the same time Shakespeare seems to be pursuing a different aim, which co-exists uncertainly with his main one. He wants to show the ladies not as detached, but as intimately involved with the young men from the very start – and not as their superiors, whether moral or emotional, but as their equals, neither obviously better nor worse.

When we first meet them, in Act II scene i, it is clearly they who are attracted to Navarre's companions, not the other way round. Their descriptions of Berowne, Dumain and Longaville are so enthusiastic that the Princess exclaims,

> God bless my ladies! Are they all in love,
> That every one her own hath garnished
> With such bedecking ornaments of praise?   (II i 77–9)

But the Princess's ladies have evidently made much less of an impact on
the young men. They make no reference to Rosaline, Katharine or
Maria when they renounce the world in the first scene, and in fact when
they meet the ladies in Act II scene i they have to find out from Boyet
what their names are. All of this puts the ladies in an emotionally
vulnerable position. But they feel doubly vulnerable and doubly
threatened because of the nature of the men to whom they are attracted.
As Maria says of Longaville,

> The only soil of his fair virtue's gloss, . . .
> Is a sharp wit match'd with too blunt a will,
> Whose edge hath power to cut, whose will still wills
> It should none spare that come within his power.
>
> > (ll. 47–51)

This charge is not made of Dumain or Berowne, but the Princess's
comment on Longaville ('Some merry mocking lord, belike'–l. 52)
becomes the keynote of the ladies' combined attitude to their suitors.
The Princess says later of the wooing-games, 'They do it but in mocking
merriment' (v ii 139), and this is the view of Berowne (with more
mockery and less merriment) that Rosaline presents at the end of the
play:

> Oft have I heard of you, my Lord Berowne,
> Before I saw you; and the world's large tongue
> Proclaims you for a man replete with mocks,
> Full of comparisons and wounding flouts.   (ll. 29–32)

Yet this is a curious speech. It is not remotely compatible with the
generous tribute to Berowne which Rosaline offers at the beginning of
the play (II i 64–76). Even less is it compatible with the Berowne that she
has actually seen. When he is with her, he is far less of a Benedick than
an Orlando; he never attempts to vent his wit on her; and among his

social equals only once – in his exasperation with Boyet in Act v – does she see him in witty abuse of another.

Rosaline is telling us one thing about Berowne, and Shakespeare has been showing us another. Her prickliness with Berowne may well stem from a sense of insecurity caused by those very feelings for him implicit in the glowing account she originally gave the Princess. Whatever the cause, the fact is that throughout much of the play Rosaline treats Berowne as someone against whom she has to be on the defensive. It manifests itself in the facade of superior witty self-possession which she exhibits in their first encounter:

> BEROWNE   Did not I dance with you in Brabant once?
> ROSALINE   Did not I dance with you in Brabant once?
> BEROWNE   I know you did.
> ROSALINE   How needless was it then to ask the question!
> BEROWNE   You must not be so quick.
> ROSALINE   'Tis long of you, that spur me with such questions.
> BEROWNE   Your wit's too hot, it speeds too fast, 'twill tire.
> ROSALINE   Not till it leave the rider in the mire.
> BEROWNE   What time o' day?
> ROSALINE   The hour that fools should ask.
> BEROWNE   Now fair befall your mask!
> ROSALINE   Fair fall the face it covers!
> BEROWNE   And send you many lovers!
> ROSALINE   Amen, so you be none.
> BEROWNE   Nay, then I will be gone.   (II i 114–28)*

Poor Berowne! This man 'replete with mocks' begins his conversation with a remark on the level of 'Do you come here often?' and finds himself sucked into a combat of wit from which he reels away wondering what hit him. Rosaline's side of the repartee is consistently aggressive, where his is defensive, and, though it is difficult to estimate tone in dialogue as artificial as this, there is perhaps something a little high-pitched and strained in her witty sallies – which in any case are not very witty.

In neither this scene nor the later ones do the ladies show much of the cool self-possession, maturity and balance with which many critics want

---

* In the Folio text Berowne here is addressing Rosaline, but in the Quarto of 1598 her speeches are assigned to Katharine. I follow most editors, though not Alexander, in accepting the Folio version. There is a discussion of this crux in the Arden edn, ed. Richard David (1951) pp. xxi–xxiii.

to credit them. What Dumain says later of Katharine, 'a fever she /
Reigns in my blood' (IV iii 91–2), seems at times to describe what is
happening to the ladies themselves. Below the level of elegant clash of
wits there are occasional glimpses of a more intense world of feeling,
which underlies and explains the ladies' consistent (and successful)
determination to put their lovers down. When the Princess urbanely
remarks, 'We are wise girls to mock our lovers so', Rosaline replies with
a speech which has, in its context, a palpably vindictive power:

> They are worse fools to purchase mocking so.
> That same Berowne I'll torture ere I go.
> O that I knew he were but in by th' week!
> How I would make him fawn, and beg, and seek,
> And wait the season, and observe the times,
> And spend his prodigal wits in bootless rhymes . . . .
>
> (v ii 59–64)

And so on: there are four more lines in similar vein. 'That same
Berowne' borders on the contemptuous, and he is to be 'tortured'
because his overtures of love are sincere, not because she thinks them a
game at her expense. On the evidence of this speech and what we see of
her throughout the play, the only thing she is qualified to teach
Berowne at the end is how to improve his capacity for 'comparisons and
wounding flouts'. The momentary quarrel between Rosaline and
Katharine in Act v scene ii has a fierceness which can be disconcerting
on stage if too much is made of it, as is indicated in this account of a
performance some years ago:

> the repartee that follows . . . was worked into a real quarrel, so that
> the Princess' 'I beshrew all shrows' had to be delivered *tutta forza* in
> order to quell it. This gave a change of tempo and colour, and showed
> us a new side of Rosaline's character, a hard shrewish side; but at this
> stage of the play neither the action nor the character had been
> sufficiently developed to bear this elaboration, and the only result
> was to turn the audience against so viperish a heroine.[16]

Few critics have commented on this side of her character, an omission
which must stem in part from the difficulty in reconciling it with what
Shakespeare is doing elsewhere.[17] The presentation of this aspect of

Rosaline gives greater depth to her portrayal and perhaps lesser dramatic consistency to the play; the gain of the one involves the comparative loss of the other.

These various elements have within them the seeds of a very different work from the one we actually have. A play which is centrally concerned with romantic themes, with attraction and hostility, with manoeuvring and the struggle to express one's real feelings, has – if, like *Love's Labour's Lost*, it is a love comedy – a natural resolution in the eventual declaration of mutual love leading to marriage. But this is not the play Shakespeare set out to write, nor the one he did write. So he tries by various ways, which are only partly successful, to redirect the play back into its original channel.

He reinforces (rather dishonestly) the impression that Navarre and his companions are perjured, thereby justifying the women's conviction that their lovers are men who make and break oaths lightly and whose word, therefore, is not to be trusted. In the masque of the Muscovites the courtiers are fooled into swearing love to the wrong ladies. Since their false oaths are the result of a mere trick, it is strange, when their 'perjury' is revealed to them, that not one of them points out the fact. The only comment is made by Berowne, and he wretchedly agrees, 'Now, to our perjury to add more terror, / We are again forsworn in will and error' (v ii 470–1). 'In *will* and error' – what is he talking about? Nevertheless, these are precisely the grounds on which the ladies reject their suitors at the end; the Princess tells Navarre, 'Your oath I will not trust' (l. 782).

That the men are genuinely in love is not open to doubt. As Dumain rather pathetically puts it, 'Our letters, madam, show'd much more than jest', and Longaville adds, 'So did our looks' (ll. 773–4). But Shakespeare has to keep us (and the ladies) from a full awareness of the fact, so that at the end of the play their uncertainty about it makes reasonable sense. Shakespeare uses several ways of scaling down our awareness that the men are in love. As each of the lovers announces himself in Act IV scene iii, Berowne acts as an ironic Chorus, distancing us from a full involvement, so that their lovelorn pining is impossible to take over-seriously. In addition Shakespeare suggests that their feelings have an element of pose about them, both the attitudes and the artificial language in which they are expressed deriving from the literary modes of Petrarchanism. Even Berowne does not escape:

Who sees the heavenly Rosaline
That, like a rude and savage man of Inde
At the first op'ning of the gorgeous east,
Bows not his vassal head and, strucken blind,
Kisses the base earth with obedient breast? . . .
A wither'd hermit, five-score winters worn,
Might shake off fifty, looking in her eye.

(IV iii 217–21, 238–9)

The more artificial the language and imagery, the less genuine must seem the passion which that language expresses. Sexually attractive maybe, but until now not even Berowne has regarded Rosaline as beautiful. The final way by which the love he and his companions feel is made to appear less than genuine and heartfelt is in their preparations for the masque of the Muscovites, which, as Boyet reports it, seem no more than the prelude to an elaborate joke:

Another with his finger and his thumb
Cried 'Via! we will do't, come what will come'.
The third he caper'd and cried 'All goes well'.
The fourth turn'd on his toe, and down he fell.
With that they all did tumble on the ground.

(V ii 111–5)

We can hardly blame the Princess for her conclusion, 'They do it but in mocking merriment' (l. 139).

The last stage in Shakespeare's attempted adjustment of our sympathies occurs during and after the episode of the Nine Worthies. Many critics have commented on the harshness and discordance of the laughter in this scene. The courtiers savage the honest efforts of the rustics, and there is something moving, because justified, in Holofernes' rebuke, 'This is not generous, not gentle, not humble' (l. 621). The ladies say nothing all this time but could be shown in performance exchanging shocked glances. When the Princess speaks, it is to offer sympathy and encouragement to the participants. On the entrance of Marcade we inevitably feel a sense of the childishness and unthinking vindictiveness of the courtiers and, correspondingly, of the reticence and consideration of the ladies. The shock of bereavement reinforces the audience's identification with the Princess and her sorrowing ladies, and we are ready (or as ready as we can be in view of everything that has gone before) to accept the impossibility of the play's ending in union.

Too much, we feel, now separates the Princess and her ladies from Navarre and his courtiers for this to be possible.

But Shakespeare is not moving his play towards a simple elegiac conclusion in which the men accept that their love must prove itself in the winter of separation before its consummation in marriage. For a start, as mentioned earlier, Katharine and Maria's mocking farewells give little cause to assume that twelve months hence they will necessarily accept the two young men who have asked for their hand. Furthermore, penances are imposed on the King and Berowne, and Berowne's comes as a shock:

> ROSALINE   . . . You shall this twelvemonth term from day to day
>   Visit the speechless sick, and still converse
>   With groaning wretches; and your task shall be,
>   With all the fierce endeavour of your wit,
>   To enforce the pained impotent to smile.
> BEROWNE   To move wild laughter in the throat of death?
>   It cannot be; it is impossible;
>   Mirth cannot move a soul in agony.   (ll. 838–45)

The contrast of Berowne's wit with the dying wretches in hospital is unexpected, violent and bizarre. I find it difficult to read Rosaline's words without hearing at the back of my mind the promise she made earlier in the same scene: 'That same Berowne I'll torture ere I go' (l. 60). 'That same Berowne' is now 'my Lord Berowne', but Rosaline has Berowne in her power, as once she felt herself to be in his. 'Fierce' seems too strong an epithet to apply to Berowne's wit, for Rosaline herself has suffered nothing at his hands. If anything, it seems rather to hint (no more) at some part of her feelings towards him. If this is present, even if it is below the surface, it is not really consistent with Shakespeare's main dramatic purpose. But it does show an imaginative fidelity to the truth of a relationship which is not, and could not have been, given full expression within the structure of the play.

V

What I have been describing amounts almost to two plays in one; an illustration – to draw on the distinction made in the opening chapter – of contradiction rather than complexity. The overt play is a satirical love-comedy in which the men are inferior to the women in character and awareness, with the result that, suitably chastened at the end, they are sent into isolation for a spell while they digest the lessons they have painfully learned. The covert one sketches the beginnings of a love-comedy of a different kind, a comedy about equals, in which the women arc as subject as the men to the disruptive effects of love, and both men and women (Berowne and Rosaline in particular) are presented as attractive if full of faults; such a love-comedy would have had a natural psychological and artistic issue in the traditional marriage festivities with which Shakespeare's other comedies end. But, as the development of *Love's Labour's Lost* makes clear, this is not what Shakespeare originally set out to write and, as I have just been arguing, he is at some pains in the second half to ensure that the play stays on its original track. The fact that this latter conception runs counter to the play's general drift and that anyway it is only intermittently present suggest that the dramatist is unlikely to have started writing the play with it in mind. Its source may lie in Shakespeare's instinct consciously or unconsciously to allow his dramatic narrative, perhaps unduly schematised in its original shape, to put down roots into the soil of a richer, more complex awareness of what human beings are and how they behave.

At this stage it may be worth raising a belated query as to whether the play's origins were in fact schematic in precisely the way they have been so far described. Can we indeed take it, as many critics have done, that the movement of *Love's Labour's Lost* signifies – and was intended to signify – a gradual progression from artifice to reality, from art to nature, from learning to experience, with in each case the former rejected in favour of the latter? So far I have taken it as self-evident. But it is arguable that the play is consciously structured in terms of opposing perspectives and viewpoints so as to invite a more finely balanced response.[18] That the possibility can be raised at all shows how hard it is to estimate Shakespeare's intentions in this play.

Complex or contradictory, *Love's Labour's Lost* would seem to be a work whose structure enlarges in order to incorporate as fully as possible the implications of the dramatic material. Much of this process may have been premeditated, but premeditation does not account for those aspects of the play I drew attention to earlier. The view of Shakespeare's dramatic structure that suggests itself is of an organic process, capable of development, growth and change, capable also of being moulded and shaped. It remains now to be seen whether this view sheds light on the way that other Shakespeare plays work.

3 Henry IV

If this study is concerned with what is most distinctive about Shakespeare, his inexhaustibility, it is appropriate to look at a play showing the dramatist at the height of his powers. *Henry IV, Part 1* is such a play. It exhibits an amplitude, ease and total mastery of dramatic technique, in which there is nothing tentative or awkward, no signs of undigested experimentation. Other plays may be more ambitious in scope – even greater – but none excels it in the confidence of its complex unfolding. *Henry IV, Part 2*, fine though it is, does not display the same degree of imaginative control and artistic intelligence. Whereas in *Part 2* we are aware of artistic problems to be solved, in *Part 1* we are not aware that problems ever existed. In both parts – as in all his plays – Shakespeare's 'shaping spirit' has to effect a resolution of competing claims. There is a tension between the external demands of form and Shakespeare's imaginative fertility, the one constantly threatening to overrun the other. The perfect consummation of form and content is achieved in the first part but not in the second.

It will become clearer later who I think has contributed most to our understanding of both plays. Critics are identifiable in terms of the approach which they exemplify, and so a judgement on the merit or otherwise of the critic implies a judgement on his particular approach. The critics I propose to look at are mainly illustrative of three approaches: historical, thematic and character. Despite their usefulness, all three are capable of misleading distortions if, instead of remaining open and flexible, allowing the possibility of complex, even contradictory, responses, they reduce the plays to a convenient, though factitious, unity. Historical criticism is most prone to this error, thematic criticism somewhat less so, and character criticism less still.

I

Shakespeare, according to Ben Jonson, 'was not of an age, but for all time'. Historical criticism insists that he may be for all time but that he was most emphatically of his age. Shakespeare did not write in a vacuum. He lived between three and four hundred years ago, and was the product of his age no less than we are the product of ours. To understand Shakespeare as he actually is we have to set him back in his own time and try to reconstruct the cultural and artistic conditions which shaped the writing of the plays.

Historical criticism is for the most part a twentieth-century phenomenon. Its origins lie mainly in the intensified scholarly interest in Shakespeare and his contemporaries in the late nineteenth century, an interest manifested in the establishment of the New Shakspere Society in 1873. They may lie partly also in a reaction to the way the second half of the nineteenth century viewed Shakespeare as a sage-like figure of almost superhuman proportions. Matthew Arnold's sonnet is typical:

> Others abide our question. Thou art free.
> We ask and ask – Thou smilest and art still,
> Out-topping knowledge.

It is salutary to turn from this tribute to Shakespeare's benign if ultimately inaccessible wisdom to seeing him as someone earning his living writing plays at the end of the sixteenth century and beginning of the seventeenth – and to see those plays as necessarily shaped by the intellectual and artistic influences of the time.

Behind historical criticism there is a further factor, which gives it a more than purely intellectual appeal. It is the desire for certainty. Because there is more written on Shakespeare than on any other writer, there is that much more disagreement. Historical criticism offers to dispel our anxieties and to furnish us with a basis for certain judgement. It will reveal the forces which shaped and conditioned Shakespeare's art, and as a result we shall have fact instead of opinion, knowledge instead of the vagaries of personal interpretation, confident certainty instead of wavering doubt. Such a claim has a most seductive appeal. But in the event historical criticism was not able to deliver what it promised. Or, more accurately, it delivered more than it was entitled to. Historical criticism nowadays is less sweeping in its claims. In order to see its place in twentieth-century Shakespeare criticism and to assess its value, it is necessary to look first at its earlier, more ambitious phase.

The main way in which scholarly knowledge and expertise were used to interpret the *Henry IV* plays was by reference to contemporary political ideas. The two parts deal with political events; therefore they are political plays; therefore it is important to know what the Elizabethans thought on political matters. So far, so reasonable. But historical critics went further. In summary form their interpretative method looked like this:

1. We must find out what the sixteenth century thought on political matters.
2. We then know what Shakespeare himself must have thought.
3. We know in addition how a contemporary audience must have reacted to his plays.
4. It is therefore clear how we, in our turn, ought to respond to them – i.e. by watching them, as far as we can, through the eyes of Shakespeare's original audience.

For a long time our sense of what the sixteenth century thought in political matters was conditioned by notions of the 'Elizabethan world picture', a phrase which has passed into common currency following the enormously influential book of that title by E. M. W. Tillyard. The world picture was one which placed a supreme value on Order or Degree, a hierarchical ordering of the cosmos with God at its highest level and inanimate matter at its lowest. Man occupied a position midway in the hierarchy; and human society represented in microcosm the larger ordering, with the king's position being analogous to that of God, and the nobles, gentlemen, yeomen and peasants extending beneath him. This paradigm represented both how things were and how they ought to be. Since everybody and everything had their appointed place in the scheme of things, it followed that obedience to the king was an absolute injunction and that rebellion – even worse, usurpation – was a grievous, unforgivable sin, unjustifiable in any circumstance. This philosophy was buttressed by what was regarded as the Tudor view of history, the so-called Tudor myth, according to which the usurpation of Richard II was paid for by a hundred years of civil strife, coming to an end only with the divinely sanctioned accession of Henry VII, the founder of the Tudor dynasty and the grandfather of Elizabeth I.

In the eyes of many critics Shakespeare's history plays reflected the Tudor insistence on the absolute necessity of obedience to the throne. The most influential was Tillyard's *Shakespeare's History Plays*, but others have pursued a similar path. Lily Campbell saw the *Henry IV* plays as expressing the Tudor doctrine on obedience embodied in the *Homilie against Disobedience and Wylfull Rebellion* of 1571, which was directed to be read out in churches, and, for that reason, in an age of compulsory church attendance, would have been familiar not only to Shakespeare but to almost every Englishman in the land:

> The king was responsible to God, both as a man, one of God's creatures, and as his vice-gerent, the representative of his divine justice. But he was responsible only to God. He was not to be judged by his subjects, and his subjects were not to decide the matter of their obedience upon the basis of the king's merits. A bad king was punishment meted out to the people for their sins, but the king was responsible to God for his sins. Rebellion was the rod of chastisement to the bad king, but the rebels were no less guilty because they were used by God. Such was the Tudor philosophy.[1]

Such too, it is suggested, was Shakespeare's. How then are we to account for the presence, and indeed the prominence, of Falstaff in both plays?

> A series of comic interludes interrupts the continuity of the historical pattern of the two parts of *Henry IV*, and because these interludes have been built about the character of Falstaff, they have obscured the history play they were meant to adorn. It is with reluctance that I relegate to an epilogue to this chapter the discussion of the immortal who has been so largely responsible for keeping the play alive in the hearts of posterity, but this is a history play, and Falstaff is historically an intruder.[2]

The next step in the historical method is that we are informed how Shakespeare's original audience would have responded to the plays. According to this group of critics the audience would have shared the assumptions of their age and, mindful of the principle of Degree, would have watched the dramatised behaviour of their betters in an appropriately acquiescent spirit. Here Tillyard, for example, writes of Hal's baiting of Francis, the Boar's Head drawer:

> It may look strange when Shakespeare in one play represents the beautiful tact of Theseus dealing with Bottom and his fellows, and in another allows his king of courtesy to be ungrateful and brutal to Francis. But Francis was a base string; Bottom a tenor string, a man in

44 SHAKESPEARE AND THE CRITICS' DEBATE

his way of intelligence and substance. Francis could not expect the same treatment. The subhuman element in the population must have been considerable in Shakespeare's day; that it should be treated almost like beasts was taken for granted.[3]

The final stage in the historical explanation of the plays is that we too should try, as far as possible, to share the preconceptions of the age that produced them. We should remind ourselves where necessary that, as Tillyard puts it, 'in matters of humanity we must not judge Shakespeare by standards of twentieth-century humanitarianism'.[4] Or if we do, we should recognise that these standards do not correspond to, and even distort, Shakespeare's original intentions and design.

Historical criticism of this kind appears to rest on a set of procedures quite embarrassingly vulnerable to awkward questions dictated less by deeper historical scholarship than by logic and common sense. On the matter of what the age believed, it is inconceivable that everyone subscribed to the doctrine of Degree in a totally unquestioning spirit. To take only one example, John Knox made it perfectly clear that his allegiance to his monarch was qualified by a higher allegiance to the Word of God as he interpreted it. Apart from such external evidence, the plays themselves are full of people who not only rebelled against their king but also felt themselves wholly justified in so doing. From this point onwards the entire edifice starts to crumble. If in principle anyone can question and ponder the implications of the official Tudor doctrine on rebellion, then (moving on to the second phase of the argument) that must include Shakespeare. It is a matter not of proving Shakespeare a political subversive, merely of giving him some intellectual freedom. To find out what he made of that freedom we have to go to the plays; they are our only evidence. And here we move on to the third stage of the argument: the claim that Elizabethan audiences 'must' have responded to certain dramatic stimuli (specifically, those to do with rebellion and loyalty) with a Pavlovian uniformity, the former unanimously ex-ecrated, the latter unanimously applauded. Simple observation of how varied people's reactions are to plays today ought to cast doubt on that assumption. Tillyard is no doubt right when he generalises about the bulk of Shakespeare's audience. We should not under-estimate the effectiveness of Tudor propaganda in an age considerably less fragmen-ted in its basic beliefs than our own; and most people of all ages in fact prefer order to disorder. But, that said, the fact remains that Elizabethan England bears only the most tenuous resemblance to

Orwell's 1984. Hence – fourth and final stage – we are not entitled to assume that what we perceive in the plays could not have been perceived by Shakespeare's audience, the odd member of which – who knows? – may have been even more perceptive and discerning than we ourselves are. Like the ideal reader, the ideal theatre-goer is a logical fiction who exists, if at all, *sub specie aeternitatis*, and there is no less, and no more, reason for locating him in Shakespeare's time than for locating him in our own.

Criticism and scholarship in the last twenty years have served to sharpen these suspicions about Tillyard's methods and conclusions. The pioneering work was done by A. P. Rossiter. He argued that the comic scenes of *Henry IV* – and especially Falstaff himself – help to create a much less simple effect than Tillyard had allowed:

> Throughout the Histories it is in the implications of the Comic that shrewd realistic thinking about men in politics – in office – in war – in plot – is exposed: realistic apprehension outrunning the medieval frame. Because the Tudor myth system of Order, Degree, etc. was too rigid, too black-and-white, too doctrinaire and narrowly moral for Shakespeare's mind: it falsified his fuller experience of men. Consequently, while employing it as FRAME, he had to undermine it, to qualify it with equivocations: to vex its application with sly or subtle ambiguities: to cast doubt on its ultimate human validity, even in situations where its principles seemed most completely applicable. His intuition told him it was *morally* inadequate.[5]

What Rossiter is saying represents a crucial insight into *Henry IV* and, simultaneously, into the reductive tendencies of earlier historical critics. All subsequent critics are in Rossiter's debt. Robert Ornstein has argued that 'What we need is not a less historical approach to the History Plays but a more rigorous methodology for that approach',[6] and he makes the point that Shakespeare's sources hardly constituted an intellectual monolith: 'Rather than an authorized version of the past, the Chronicles offered Elizabethan artists a fascinating hodge-podge of significant and trivial facts, of shrewd judgements and fantastic opinions, eclectically gathered and often uncritically repeated.'[7]

Tillyard's central thesis has nevertheless had an extraordinarily potent and lasting influence. In an essay with the splendidly gestural title 'Put Away the World-Picture'[8] Herbert Howarth points out how it has had the effect of imposing an intellectual straitjacket on many students' response to the plays. Earlier critics such as Tillyard seemed to say to Shakespeare what Hal patronisingly says to Poins: 'thou art a blessed fellow to think as every man thinks. Never a man's thought in the world keeps the road-way better than thine' (*Pt 2*, ii ii 52–5). The compelling argument against traditional historical criticism is that it so totally fails to explain how a dramatist of such blinkered intellect and limited emotional and imaginative sympathies could have survived his age for nearly four hundred years.

Another influential historical approach has been that which sets Shakespeare in the context of the dramatic conventions of his age. The conventional nature of sixteenth- and seventeenth-century drama was insisted on by M. C. Bradbrook and Una Ellis-Fermor.[9] In part at least this was in response to William Archer's *The Old Drama and the New* celebrating modern naturalistic prose drama and dismissing the verse drama of the Elizabethan period. Archer complained of the earlier drama's imprecision in matters of space and time and its use of such inherently implausible assumptions as that asides can never be overheard and a character's disguise is always impenetrable. The reply made to Archer was: implausible or not, they happen to be conventions adopted by the dramatists of the period (including Shakespeare); the fact that they were widely used indicates that they posed no problems for the original audiences; because they were acceptable to audiences then, they need present no problems to audiences now; to complain of their presence is to misunderstand and misjudge the significance of the drama of which Shakespeare formed a part.

There is a general similarity between this line of argument and the one I have just been criticising. In both cases relative judgements are transformed into absolute ones: if something is good enough for the Elizabethans it is good enough for us. In both cases there is a reluctance to grant Shakespeare very much independence, whether of mind or art; he is implicitly congratulated for conforming to the intellectual standards and artistic practices of his age. In both cases it is precisely the nature and degree of this conformity that need clarification.

A dramatic convention can be said to exist only after observing correspondences and similarities in the works of several dramatists. Once observed there is a temptation for critics to ignore differences of treatment and to refrain from asking, 'How well or badly is the convention employed in this particular play?' Its use does not by itself confer artistic merit on the work. Some dramatists handle their conventional material more skilfully than others. In this respect, unsurprisingly, Shakespeare can be shown to be a finer craftsman than his contemporaries. His superiority lies largely in the trouble he takes to give his conventional material an appearance of plausibility; he does not make inordinate demands on our willing suspension of disbelief. The point was well recognised by Archer, who exempted Shakespeare from most of his strictures on Elizabethan drama.[10]

The less a convention offends our notions of common-sense plausibility, the less we need to invoke the term 'convention' in the first place. The result is that sometimes there is uncertainty over whether an element of convention is present at all. An example is Hal's soliloquy near the beginning of *Part 1*, 'I know you all' (I ii 188–210). Is it meant to be psychologically revealing, or is it a piece of impersonal choric commentary in which Hal steps momentarily out of character to address the audience? S. L. Bethell claims it is the latter:

> On the naturalistic approach, one is shocked to note that Henry has apparently no affection for his boon companions; we should prefer genuine wild oats to such calculating and unprincely behavior. . . . We must not take the speech naturalistically at all, so as to accuse Henry of a deliberate plan to secure favorable publicity. . . . An audience used to speeches addressed directly to themselves, in which they are, as it were, taken into the confidence of a stage character, would understand Prince Henry's soliloquy in this way, as an objective statement of the facts; they would not think of it as implying this or that unfortunate blemish in his princely nature.[11]

The kind of 'naturalistic' scrutiny to which Bethell objects is exemplified by John Palmer:

> Henry may mean precisely what he says; in that case he consorts with inferior persons from pure policy; he is misconducting himself in Eastcheap, so that later on, in Westminster, he may startle and impress the world with his good behaviour. Perhaps, however, he is merely trying, with false reasons, to justify his present way of life; in that case he combines an honest liking for vulgar society with a sharp sense of his own superior station. In either event what becomes of the prince of good fellows? Henry, if he means what he says, is a false good fellow who does nothing without premeditation. If, on the contrary,

he is merely looking for a reason to be merry with his friends, surely he might have found a better one. To plead that he is permitting their base contagious clouds to smother up his beauty in order that he may shine all the more brightly when they have served his turn is not the sort of excuse which would have suggested itself to a really good companion.[12]

Palmer and Bethell represent two different approaches to this speech. Mutually exclusive though they may seem, an attempt to synthesise them has been made by Daniel Seltzer; he sees the soliloquy as expressing

a technique uniquely Shakespearian: that of expression, moment by moment, of an inner state and an immediate present time. The first soliloquy, considered in this way, is indeed in the long tradition of self-descriptive speeches in Tudor drama, and very conventionally so – but with a difference. . . . Hal's soliloquy is spoken in direct reaction to the scene at the end of which it occurs . . . 'I know you all, and will awhile uphold / The unyoked humour of your idleness'. The present thought springs from the present stimulus, and so does all that follows it, necessarily self-descriptive, but necessarily describing a plan, if we can call it that, which projects Hal's self-experience only as far as this part of his journey through the play can have carried it.[13]

The degree of conventionality in the speech is clearly a matter of debate. Ornstein, who, as noted earlier, is opposed only to misplaced historicism, comes down firmly on Palmer's side:

It seems to me preferable to interpret the soliloquy as soliloquy rather than to turn Shakespeare into a blunderer who did not realize the chilling effect of Hal's contemptuous lines about his comrades and who failed to see how Hal's diction and metaphors associate his calculated redemption with the crassness of commodity and sharp business practices. . . . Far from being a neutral choric announcement, Hal's soliloquy in the tavern strikes the keynote of his characterization . . . fascinating but not endearing; not quite the paragon some would have him nor the heartless prig others see.[14]

One final point. Historical criticism's original appeal was its claim to provide greater objectivity, to free us from the vagaries of personal interpretation. It is worth pointing out then that Bethell's historical account subserves a prior critical interpretation: Hal *is* morally impeccable, *therefore* his first soliloquy must be an impersonal choric statement rather than a personal revealing utterance of a faintly disturbing kind. It is not the fact of covert critical bias as such to which I want to draw attention. It is that the particular bias exhibited by Bethell reflects such an over-simplified and inadequate view of the plays.

II

'Theme' is a highly useful term in talking about Shakespeare – so useful in fact that it is surprising to realise that it has gained wide currency only fairly recently. One wonders how we got along without it. It serves to focus our minds on what a play seems fundamentally to be about. Its usefulness is indicated by the frequency with which it now crops up not only in books and articles but also – as an inevitable consequence for students – in essay topics and exam questions. The addition of this term to our critical vocabulary has not, however, been simple gain. Discussion of Shakespeare in terms of his themes has its attendant dangers; the main one, as with historical criticism, is its encouragement to take an over-simplified view of the plays being discussed.

J. F. Danby presents a grimly disenchanted view of the world of *Henry IV*:

> What we have called Authority (or Power) and Appetite Dr Tillyard calls Order and Disorder (or Riot) and accounts for *Henry IV, Parts 1 and 2* in these terms. Dr Tillyard makes an absolute distinction between the two. Order is a real absolute value, Riot a real immorality. Hal turns his back irrevocably on Riot and is converted to the party of My Lord Chief Justice – *Justitia*. The view proposed here as an alternative to Dr Tillyard's makes no such absolute distinction between Hal and Falstaff. The opposition into which they are thrown is an appearance rather than a reality. When Hal moves from Eastcheap to the Court, from Falstaff to My Lord Chief Justice, he is merely leaving the unofficial sphere of Elizabethan life for the official sphere. The two are different, and require different habits. But the difference is not essentially a moral difference. It is a difference of social function. On the view proposed here Authority

(or Power) and Appetite occupy the same plane. Both are essential to the running of the Elizabethan state. Equally immoral, both collaborate to maintain an iniquitous world.[15]

Now the theme of Power and Appetite, as Danby defines it, may tell us a lot about the plays, especially *Part 2*, but it does not tell us everything. Neither the phrase itself nor Danby's exegesis encompasses the full range of tonal effects in the two plays. In *Part 1* at least, Shakespeare seems to find, like Dr Johnson's friend, that, however much he tries to be philosophical about life, cheerfulness keeps breaking in.

This kind of reservation indicates the core of the problem. Themes, however formulated, are by their very nature abstract and general, and Shakespeare's drama is particular, concrete, richly complex and multi-faceted; it is also, as Rossiter pointed out, ambivalent. The plays put up a remarkable degree of resistance to having their significance summed up in a phrase. Faced with such abundance the thematic critic has a virtually impossible task; he cannot hope to get it all in. Any formulation, such as Danby's, is bound to schematise the play, to abstract from it, and hence to distort it to a greater or lesser degree. Another aspect of the problem lies in the assumption made by thematic criticism about the way the plays came to be written. Is Shakespeare's main interest in general questions which he explores in dramatic form using imagined characters and situations? Or is it initially, though not exclusively, in those very characters and situations? Does Shakespeare's imagination, that is to say, work from the general to the particular or from the particular to the general? Although the question is finally unanswerable, thematic criticism is prone to assume the former rather than the latter, an assumption which means it runs the constant risk of seeming thin-blooded, of offering us the shell for the substance, a formula in place of the imaginative reality. What a work is, sprawling and untidy as it often seems, is more important than what it may be said to be about. As [I believe] Kenneth Tynan put it once, replying to a woman who wanted to know what were the main themes of *Hamlet*, 'Themes, madam? Nay, it *is*. I know not themes.'

The Shakespeare of Derek Traversi is much given to probing and analysing general matters. While the centre of the *Henry IV* plays is located in the moral development of Hal's character, the process itself illustrates a more general concern. The question we come increasingly to ask ourselves as we follow Hal's career is, 'What are the personal, as distinct from the political, qualities that go to the making of a king?' The answer Shakespeare gives, according to Traversi, is that 'success in politics implies a moral loss, the sacrifice of more attractive qualities in the distinctively personal order'.[16] Traversi's documentation is detailed, painstaking and thorough – even oppressively so. On a rough count his study of the two parts of *Henry IV* is as long as the plays themselves. Within that space he goes a long way to relating what he takes to be the plays' main theme to the plays themselves as they unfold scene by scene. But one has on the one hand the frequent, and slightly wearying, sense that the last drop of meaning is being extracted from the text, and on the other (paradoxically) that there is more to the plays than Traversi acknowledges.

A critic who has a sharp sense of the problems involved in thematic discussion is L. C. Knights.

> These are not 'abstract themes', 'philosophical concepts', or 'bare general propositions'; they represent a set or slant of interest that springs from and engages the concern of the personality as a whole; and although that, in turn, is far from being simply a concern for *this* man in *this* action – for it has to do with fundamental and lasting aspects of the human situation that are focused in the given case – it is only through the particular action, the precise articulation of a work of art, that it can be clarified and brought to expression. . . . What they point towards is an organisation of experience so living and complex that when we are engaged in it, living it to the full extent of our powers, we have no need of token definitions. It is only later, when we wish to give others some account of the experience to which we have responded – or, better, the experience that we have undergone – that we say, hesitatingly, 'It was about some such matters as this. Look!'[17]

For Knights the theme that dominates the second part of *Henry IV* is time and change. Considered as a summing-up of the play this is, as he would admit, a distinctly 'bare general proposition', and a vague one at that. But his commentary on the play amplifies and develops what he means, so that gradually we see the relevance of the stated theme to the texture of the play:

> *2 Henry IV*, a tragi-comedy of human frailty, is about the varied aspects of mutability – age, disappointment and decay. . . . Act III, the central act, has only two scenes, one at court, one in Gloucestershire,

and the second succeeds the first without a break. With the King's words still in our ears we are given (among other things) one of the most superb variations in English literature on the theme of *le temps perdu*. Act III, scene ii, like the later Cotswold scenes, is firmly rooted in the actual. Life is going on in this little bit of rural England, and will go on, for all the wars and civil wars now and to come – the smith must be paid, the hade land sown with red wheat, and the well-chain mended. That life is vividly present to us, built up little by little with unobtrusive art. But the scene is drenched in memory. In the first fifty lines, as Shallow recalls the poor pranks of his mad days at Clement's Inn, the exploits of young Jack Falstaff who is now old, and of old Double who is dead, we are at least as much aware of the past (and of the fact that it *is* the past) as of anything in the present.[18]

The complaint made already that themes tend by their very nature to be abstract and generalised and hence to falsify the play could be pressed a little further. At one level it is no doubt true that everything we say about a Shakespeare play is an abstraction which presumably falsifies it to some degree. But thematic criticism is different from other forms of Shakespeare criticism – imagery analysis, for instance. Images at least are there: if one has the inclination and stamina, they can even be counted as a way of assessing their total effect. But themes are another matter. They cannot be counted. They are invisible. Themes are *our* constructs, rather than something given to us by the play. Not merely are they not there in the same way as images, but the question can at least be asked in what sense they are there at all.

Themes express the significance that *we* find in the plays; they are about what the plays mean to *us*. But how can we be sure that what they mean to us corresponds with what they meant for Shakespeare? Is there not a danger that we read significance into the plays rather than elicit significance from them? Such a possibility follows directly from the nature of drama itself, which lacks the novel's traditional third-person narrator or the omnipresent 'I' of lyric poetry. And Shakespeare's plays exhibit this impersonality to an unusual degree. If Shakespeare is concerned about the significance of the action in which his imagined characters are involved, he is notoriously reluctant to indicate what that significance is. We rarely feel his elbow in our ribs, ensuring that we get the message. He has no explicit Chorus to act as his mouthpiece; and characteristically, in the few plays that do have a Chorus–*Henry V*, say– the Chorus's point of view on the events he introduces is merely one among many. The use of multiple viewpoints explains much of Shakespeare's reticence, inexplicitness and seeming impersonality; and it is these features of his work with which thematic criticism has somehow to come to terms.

The need to tread delicately is reinforced when we reflect that thematic criticism almost inevitably has a moralistic bent. Both the desire to extract a moral from Shakespeare's plays and a vexatious sense of the difficulty in actually finding one are expressed by Dr Johnson. 'He sacrifices virtue to convenience, and is so much more careful to please than to instruct that he seems to write without any moral purpose.' On the ending of *As You Like It* he writes, 'By hastening to the end of his work, Shakespeare suppressed the dialogue between the usurper and the hermit and lost an opportunity of exhibiting a moral lesson in which he might have found matter worthy of his highest powers.'[19] Johnson's desire for an edifying moral lesson no doubt had some part in his preference for Nahum Tate's adaptation of *King Lear* over Shakespeare's original. With all tribulations behind them, Edgar concludes the play by announcing to his recently betrothed Cordelia – and, by extension, to Lear, Gloster and the other assembled lords,

> Thy bright example shall convince the world
> (Whatever storms of Fortune are decreed)
> That Truth and Vertue shall at last succeed.[20]

As uplifting and explicitly rendered a moral as one could hope to find.

Moralistic criticism, whether of Shakespeare or of literature in general, is a touchy subject; the term 'moralistic' is itself more than faintly pejorative. As a first comment on the matter it is worth making the fairly neutral point that even the historical critics dealt with in the preceding section could be regarded as moralistic. The quotation from Danby on pp. 49–50 makes it clear that he is following in the steps of E. M. W. Tillyard, and is merely altering his terminology in order to give a shift of emphasis of Tillyard's interpretation: for 'Order and Disorder' read 'Authority and Appetite'. 'The theme of Order and Disorder in the histories' is not different in kind from 'the theme of Authority and Appetite'. Both are themes; both suggest the attitudes – moral, necessarily – which Shakespeare is presumed to be taking to the characters and events of the plays. 'The theme of honour in *Henry IV, Part 1*' is again a moral issue. So too is 'the theme of divine right in

Richard II'. The elucidation of any of these themes would involve showing how Shakespeare sets the ways in which men do behave in a larger context of how they ought to behave.

But this of course is acceptable. Historical critics usually manage to keep Shakespeare firmly penned in the sixteenth century. Where Danby, Traversi and Knights (in that order) take increasing risks is in suggesting that Shakespeare's intelligence, imagination and sensibility are such that his plays contain insights about human nature that are as valid today as they were then. It is this particular claim that causes stirrings of unease. One fear is that approaching Shakespeare in such a spirit can lead to sacrificing his art on the altar of his morality. In other words, critics such as the ones just mentioned resemble Kenneth Tynan's questioner: more interested in what the plays are about than in what they are, prisoners of a blinkered didacticism, unable to respond to art as art. They use Shakespeare's plays for the moral nutriment to be derived from them, turning Shakespeare into a sermoniser and moralist rather than a playwright. They furthermore seem to claim a remark-able access to Shakespeare's innermost thoughts and assume the right to interpret them to the rest of us – to interpret, indeed, Shakespeare's moral development as it is revealed through the plays.

L. C. Knights, who is simultaneously the most modest and the most ambitious of this group of critics, is also the most vulnerable to these criticisms. Here is part of what he has to say at the end of his discussion of *Henry IV, Part 2*:

> I hope this does not seem like putting Shakespeare on the rack of a demand for a moral at any price. Shakespeare never explicitly points a moral; and it will be some years before he fully reveals in terms of the awakened imagination why those that follow their noses are led by their eyes, or what it really means to be the fool of time. For the moment we are only concerned with the direction that his developing insight is taking; and it seems to me that what is coming into consciousness is nothing less than an awareness of how men make the world that they inhabit, an understanding of the relation between what men are and the kind of perceptions they have about the nature of things.[21]

This extract (I hope not wrenched too arbitrarily from its context) will strike some readers as less literary criticism than part of a stage-by-stage tour of Shakespeare's spiritual development in which the plays are merely convenient signposts; an unfair reaction in some ways, but understandable.

The objections to such speculation are of two kinds. The first is that it is inherently unprovable, and because unprovable can lead to mere fantasising. The second objection, often strongly felt though not always clearly formulated, is that in this kind of criticism it is very easy to achieve the wrong tone. While everyone acknowledges in a general way Shakespeare's breadth of human sympathy and understanding, critics who offer to talk about his moral attitudes must not give the impression that it is their own quasi-Shakespearean sensitivity and moral awareness that qualify them to interpret the dramatist to his readers. As T. J. B. Spencer put it, 'it is a natural impulse delightedly to discover, and to reveal to the world, that Shakespeare was as wise and perceptive as ourselves'.[22] L. C. Knights, I should add, does not seem to me to commit such a failure of tact, but this kind of criticism has to guard against seeming to do so.

To sum up, the problems about thematic criticism stem from two facts: that themes deal as a rule with the moral significance of Shakespeare's plays; and that the plays' themes are in practice highly elusive – so much so that Dr Johnson wondered at times whether they were there at all. The result is that thematic critics are capable of false and distorting over-emphasis, of making the plays seem more self-conscious and explicit than in fact they are, in extreme cases of inventing significance, or even of projecting their own moral pre-occupations, standards and beliefs on to Shakespeare's work. Every critic has to make his own assessment of just how far Shakespeare's hand is detectable in the plays, guiding and directing his response, suggesting conclusions. Too far in one direction and Shakespeare disappears from the plays altogether, indifferent to the world he has created, expressing nothing, affirming nothing. Too far in the other (a direction taken by some thematic criticism) and Shakespeare becomes almost a preacher, more concerned with uplift than with art. On this point there will always be disagreement: neither indifferent nor dogmatic, Shakespeare nevertheless eludes convenient summary; and it seems a matter of prudence that interpretations of the moral themes of the plays should reflect something of Shakespeare's own undogmatic spirit.

III

Criticism of Shakespeare has its fashions like everything else, and in the course of this century character criticism has been in, out, and now seems to be in again. The approach involves not merely the discussion of characters as they appear in the plays, but also the tacit assumption that in the creation of vivid, memorable, well-differentiated characters lies Shakespeare's distinctive achievement. Certainly this assumption has been present in the popular view of the plays for a very long time; it represents the initial point of contact with Shakespeare for people not necessarily concerned to make him the object of intensive study. The first *Complete Works* I can remember looking at had in its inside cover a picture of the dramatist in beard and bardic robes gesturing in proprietorial fashion to a throng of people standing behind and to one side of him: Lear, Malvolio, Titania and Bottom, Hamlet, Rosalind and many others – including of course Falstaff.

This view of the plays as Shakespeare's portrait gallery has a long history. At least two hundred years in fact, for in 1777 appeared the first full-length study of a Shakespeare character, Maurice Morgann's *An Essay on the Dramatic Character of Sir John Falstaff*, the primary concern of which was to defend Falstaff from the charge of being a constitutional coward. The nineteenth century was, however, the golden age of character criticism. Two factors probably accounted for this. One was the general ethos of Romanticism, with its emphasis on the individual. But a more pervasive and significant influence was that of the novel, which became the dominant literary form in the nineteenth century. The novel provided realistic, vivid and detailed studies of individual characters, often introduced by a brief biography and followed (as in *Middlemarch*) with a postscript indicating what happened to them after the main action of the novel. The illusion was created that characters have a life outside the confines of the actual novel, the illusion of documentary realism. This assumption had its effect in some of the offshoots of Shakespeare criticism in the nineteenth century, such as Mary Cowden Clarke's *Girlhood of Shakespeare's Heroines*, a work of innocuous charm but without much direct relevance to the plays.

In 1904 appeared A. C. Bradley's *Shakespearean Tragedy*. Its publication came to be regarded as the high point of character criticism, and this form of criticism in fact was often referred to, rather disparagingly, as 'the Bradley approach'. In many ways this was unfair. Bradley provided a seriously argued investigation into the nature of Shakespearean tragedy, and his comments on the individual plays go much beyond mere discussion of character. Nevertheless, the appendices to his lectures do seem based on the assumption that characters in Shakespeare can be studied in exactly the same way as people in real life: Note A – Events before the opening of the action in *Hamlet*; Note B – Where was Hamlet at the time of his father's death?; Note C – Hamlet's age; and so on. The proper reply to a question such as 'Where was Hamlet at the time of his father's death?' is that we don't know; we have no means of knowing (there is no independent biography of Hamlet for us to consult); and we don't really care (the question is irrelevant to our experience of the play). But the fact that such questions could be asked and the possible answers pursued with such assiduity suggested that character criticism was over-reaching itself.

A reaction was bound to come. When it took place, it followed in part from a growing awareness of the conventional nature of Elizabethan character portrayal, discussed earlier in this chapter. At the same time critical attention was being diverted away from questions of character altogether into more fruitful areas. In 1933 L. C. Knights delivered to the Shakespeare Association a lecture with the title 'How Many Children Had Lady Macbeth?' combining an energetic attack on Bradleyism with some equally energetic propaganda for the new belief in the controlling importance of Shakespeare's language: 'A Shakespeare play is a dramatic poem.'[23] The view of Shakespeare to which Knights is indebted here is that of G. Wilson Knight, whose *The Wheel of Fire* is quoted approvingly:

> We should not look for perfect verisimilitude to life, but rather see each play as an expanded metaphor, by means of which the original vision has been projected into forms roughly correspondent with actuality, conforming thereto with greater or less exactitude according to the demands of its nature. . . . The persons, ultimately, are not human at all, but purely symbols of a poetic vision.[24]

Significantly, when Wilson Knight revised *The Wheel of Fire* for its fourth edition in 1949 he deleted that last sentence and in a Prefatory Note made a guardedly complimentary reference to Bradley. Of such shifts of emphasis are swings of pendulums made and unmade.

Despite the influential work in the 1930s by Wilson Knight, Caroline Spurgeon and Wolfgang Clemen, analysing Shakespeare's language and poetic structure with a thoroughness it had not received before, several critics felt that traditional discussion of character still had its uses – for instance, H. B. Charlton, whose approach to *Love's Labour's Lost* was briefly considered in the last chapter, and John Palmer, whose *Political Characters of Shakespeare* in 1945 combined a genial tone with great shrewdness and incisiveness. Recently the diffused influence of Bradley and the much more specific influence of Palmer are detectable in Robert Ornstein's *A Kingdom for a Stage*. It would be too pat to say that Ornstein brings the wheel full circle;[25] but the detailed attention paid to Hal, Bolingbroke and Hotspur (surprisingly little to Falstaff) indicates his awareness of the personalities that flesh out the political dimension of the play. Despite or because of its traditional quality, his book is consistently illuminating. The connections, where made, are unforced and unlaboured: after suggesting that 'all the world's a stage in the second tetralogy', he makes the neat point that, 'Injured innocence and moral indignation are among the most popular roles in *Part 1*. Falstaff assumes them with Hal, Hal with Falstaff, Henry with the Percies and the Percies with Henry.'[26]

That the case against character criticism had been over-stated is evident from both Wilson Knight's own belated recognition and this extract from 'How Many Children Had Lady Macbeth?'

> In the mass of Shakespeare criticism there is not a hint that 'character' – like 'plot', 'rhythm', 'construction' and all our other critical counters – is merely an abstraction from the total response in the mind of the reader or spectator.[27]

Well, yes, 'character' is an abstraction, if one wants to call it that. But one crucial distinction between the characters of a play and these other critical counters is that characters can be clearly identified; Shakespeare has told us their names; he has not identified his rhythm, construction – or even themes, as I mentioned earlier – with equal explicitness. We look *for* themes, we look *at* characters. So it follows that we quite naturally have a lot to say about the characters, since they are what catches our attention first, before we think about the significance of other aspects. The attempt recommended by Wilson Knight to absorb the characters' individuality back into the totality of one's experience of the play, the total poetic–dramatic vision, has certain dangers. It can lead not to a deepening but to a thinning of one's experience. To discover that characters are 'symbolic personifications'

(Wilson Knight's phrase again) is not always a positive gain. In the 1930s Falstaff was once described as a 'walking symbol'. If that were said now, it would invite the reply that anyone can come up with a symbol; it takes a Shakespeare to create a Falstaff.

The practical value of character criticism varies from play to play. Because Shakespeare's plays are different, certain approaches will be more fruitful in one play than in another. If there exists a large body of character criticism of *Henry IV*, it is because the two plays invite it. They present us, whether as readers or audience, with a broad sweep of English life, and we respond with a lively interest to all its manifestations, not only to the four or five main characters who dominate the action but also to the host of minor characters, none of whom we would willingly sacrifice. Dr Johnson phrased it most memorably, writing here about Pistol's final exit in *Henry V*:

> The comic scenes of *The History of Henry the Fourth* and *Fifth* are now at an end, and all the comic personages are now dismissed. Falstaff and Mrs. Quickly are dead; Nym and Bardolph are hanged; Gadshill was lost immediately after the robbery; Poins and Peto have vanished since, one knows not how; and Pistol is now beaten into obscurity. I believe every reader regrets their departure.[28]

Characters in other plays, however, do not always stimulate this degree of warm involvement, and are not intended to. The formality and complexity of the plot of *The Comedy of Errors*, with the multiple mistaken identities resulting from two sets of identical twin brothers, preclude any subtle differentiation of character. The way the characters are presented is more external, our relationship with them less intimate. The plays are the best guide as to which approach is most productive, and within each play the limitations on the various characters' dramatic life are sufficiently indicated by the characters themselves, if we have the patience and imaginative tact to follow where they lead – and no further. The limits of legitimate analysis and speculation are not in practice difficult to discern, except where, as Bradley put it at the end of his essay on Falstaff, Shakespeare bestows on some of his characters that 'inexplicable touch of infinity'[29] present in Hamlet, Macbeth, Cleopatra, and Falstaff himself.

IV

Character criticism is potentially more responsive to the element of ambiguity in Shakespeare's work than historical and thematic criticism, since they are prone to elide those features of a play which do not fit what seems at times a pre-determined pattern. Character criticism of course has its excesses, which must be guarded against. But the most damaging one is not the old-fashioned keenness to fill in biographical gaps. It is the failure to rise to the distinctive complexity of what Shakespeare has created, and in this respect its failures are no different from those of the other two.

Although Falstaff may seem too easy a subject on which to prove the point, it is instructive to see some of the difficulties critics have had in coming to terms with him. The most celebrated summary is that of Dr Johnson:

> But Falstaff, unimitated, unimitable Falstaff, how shall I describe thee? Thou compound of sense and vice; of sense which may be admired but not esteemed, of vice which may be despised but hardly detested. Falstaff is a character loaded with faults, and with those faults which naturally produce contempt. He is a thief and a glutton, a coward and a boaster, always ready to cheat the weak and prey upon the poor; to terrify the timorous and insult the defenceless. At once obsequious and malignant, he satirizes in their absence those whom he lives by flattering. He is familiar with the prince only as an agent of vice, but of this familiarity he is so proud as not only to be supercilious and haughty with common men but to think his interest of importance to the Duke of Lancaster. Yet the man thus corrupt, makes himself necessary to the prince that despises him, by the most pleasing of all qualities, perpetual gaiety, an unfailing power of exciting laughter, which is the more freely indulged as his wit is not of the splendid or ambitious kind but consists in easy escapes and sallies of levity, which make sport but raise no envy. It must be observed that he is stained with no enormous or sanguinary crimes, so that his licentiousness is not so offensive but that it may be borne for his mirth.
>
> The moral to be drawn from this representation is that no man is more dangerous than he that, with a will to corrupt, hath the power to please; and that neither wit nor honesty ought to think themselves safe with such a companion when they see Henry seduced by Falstaff.[30]

It is not so much the Prince as Johnson himself who is in danger of being seduced; one suspects that he enjoyed Falstaff's intoxicating presence more than Hal ever did. But there is no doubt that he is aware of being pulled in opposing directions; and it is a mark of how fully Johnson responded that he should register these contradictory aspects of Falstaff's character without sacrificing one to the other.

Later critics, though, have not always been so successful. Bradley's account dismisses the moral significance of everything Falstaff does, and offers instead an eloquent, even rhapsodic defence of 'the immortal Falstaff, a character almost purely humorous, and therefore no subject for moral judgements. . . . They are to him absurd; and to reduce a thing *ad absurdum* is to reduce it to nothing and to walk about free and rejoicing.'[31] J. Dover Wilson, in contrast, felt that Bradley had been much too indulgent to the fat fraud, and is determined not to be so taken in. Nevertheless, his approach, whether viewed as character criticism or as a form of historical criticism, is almost as one-sided as Bradley's:

> Hal associates Falstaff in turn with the Devil of the miracle play, the Vice of the morality, and the Riot of the interlude, when he calls him 'that villainous abominable misleader of Youth, that old white-bearded Satan', 'that reverend Vice, that grey Iniquity, that father Ruffian, that Vanity in years', and 'the tutor and the feeder of my riots'. . . . Shakespeare's audience enjoyed the fascination of Prince Hal's 'white-bearded Satan' for two whole days, as perhaps no character on the world's stage had ever been enjoyed before. But they knew, from the beginning, that the reign of this marvellous Lord of Misrule must have an end, that Falstaff must be rejected by the Prodigal Prince, when the time for reformation came. And they no more thought of questioning or disapproving of that finale, than their ancestors would have thought of protesting against the Vice being carried off to Hell at the end of the interlude.[32]

One's misgivings about the drift of Dover Wilson's argument crystallise when we read a few lines further on, 'After all, Falstaff *is* "a devil . . . in the likeness of an old fat man".' To this there is only one reply: no, he isn't. When Hal called him that, he was not stating a literal fact, and it is inconceivable that even the play's original audience thought he was.

Dover Wilson has much that is perceptive, particularly on the differences between Falstaff in *Part 1* and Falstaff in *Part 2*, but, ironically, he is at his best when least dependent on his historical method. His tendency to simplify the play's effects is illustrated by his view of Falstaff's two meetings in *Part 2* with the Lord Chief Justice. Their encounters, scarcely essential from the point of view of the plot, Dover Wilson regards as the symbolic confrontation of Riot and Law, in which Falstaff is clearly seen to come off worse. So in a sense it is. But Ornstein, without undermining this view entirely, suggests other ways of looking at their meetings:

> The shabbiness of Falstaff's way of life in *Part 2* is emphasized by his encounters with the Lord Chief Justice, who has the dignity of his office and an honorable age. A model of propriety, the Chief Justice would be perfectly suited to lecture Falstaff were it not for the self-righteousness of his manner. He would have Falstaff confess his age and prepare for his end; but though he objects to old men like Falstaff drinking and whoring, he does not object to old men like Falstaff fighting at Gaultree Forest so that the respectable can kiss 'my Lady Peace' safely at home. When Falstaff fondles Doll in the Boar's Head tavern, we can laugh at the joke of an aging lecher whose whore unpacks her store of professional endearments. Or we can hear in Doll's words a touch of affection and sympathy lacking in the homilies of her betters.[33]

The balance between enjoyment, sympathy and condemnation in our attitude to Falstaff is a fine and shifting one, and it is critics such as Rossiter and Ornstein, responsive to the ambiguity of Shakespeare's treatment, who are most likely to get it right. Shakespeare's dramatic effects, that is, are complex but not muddled; we are not called upon simultaneously to affirm contrary propositions. But there is one area where the views expressed do seem to be mutually exclusive. I refer to the old chestnut: is Falstaff a coward?

While it is a far less crucial issue than it was once taken to be, it cannot be entirely glossed over. Falstaff himself is scarcely indifferent on the matter; in *Part 1* Hal twice calls him a coward, and on both occasions he vehemently denies it.[34] Anyway, the critic has a responsibility to explain what to the ordinary eye is a mass of conflicting evidence, some of which suggests that Falstaff is a coward and some of which suggests the reverse. In the past there has been much heated argument on the subject. The eighteenth century generally and Dr Johnson in particular were convinced that Falstaff was a coward. Maurice Morgann argued that this was an unjustified slur on Falstaff's reputation. In this he was later supported by Bradley. One solution to the problem is to accept that the evidence is simply irreconcilable. This is what Dover Wilson does when he comments on Falstaff's unconcernedly falling asleep behind the curtain while Hal keeps away the sheriff's men who have come to arrest him: 'That he should sleep so soundly is itself the final answer to the Prince's slanderous story of the events on Gad's Hill: the two Falstaffs cannot be the same man.'[35]

What we have to look for is some more or less consistent centre to his personality which binds together the various contradictions; and it is revealed, I believe, in Falstaff's characteristic speech patterns. In the extracts that follow the first speech is by Poins, the rest are all Falstaff's:

. . . for [Falstaff], if he fight longer than he sees reason, I'll forswear arms. (*Pt 1*, I ii 177–9)

I deny your major. If you will deny the sheriff, so; if not, let him enter. If I become not a cart as well as another man, a plague on my bringing up! (II iv 478–80)

Well, if Percy be alive, I'll pierce him. If he do come in my way, so; if he do not, if I come in his willingly, let him make a carbonado of me. I like not such grinning honour as Sir Walter hath. Give me life, which if I can save, so; if not, honour comes unlook'd for, and there's an end. (v iii 53–9)

There is Percy [*throwing the body down*]; if your father will do me any honour, so; if not, let him kill the next Percy himself. (v iv 138–40)

If I may be believ'd, so; if not, let them that should reward valour bear the sin upon their own heads. (ll. 147–9)

If the young dace be a bait for the old pike, I see no reason in the law of nature but I may snap at him. Let time shape, and there an end. (*Pt 2*, III ii 321–3)

These are almost all a series of hypothetical statements: if so and so happens, then . . . .[36] This is the language of the practised manipulator who realises that he can shape events but not control them; five times the hypothetical situation is accepted happily or resignedly with a simple 'so'; each time it is followed by the acknowledgement that every hypothetical possibility has its converse: 'if not, . . . '. Twice he commits himself to the future with the shrugging casualness of 'and there's an end'. The verbal similarities here reveal a consistency of outlook in Falstaff. He both actively manipulates and passively accepts. He is self-interested, canny and stoical. His way is to improvise a situation, moment by moment even, for his own ends while weighing the possible consequences, good or bad. If the likely consequences are unwelcome, he will avoid them if he can; if they prove unavoidable they must be endured. This underlying philosophy gives him the minimum nerve required to improvise the situation in the first place, and to accept the unwished for consequences if they are genuinely inescapable. Ascribing to Falstaff a centre of gravity of this kind helps to make sense of his seeming both cowardly and courageous by turns. It supplies a basic consistency to such incidents as his running away at Gad's Hill, his feigning death at Shrewsbury, and his almost comic capture of Coleville of the Dale at Gaultree Forest.

Finally in this discussion of the ambiguities in Shakespeare's presentation of character in the *Henry IV* plays, I should like to look briefly at Hal. He has at different times been vilified as a cold-hearted, self-justifying prig and celebrated as Shakespeare's ideal monarch. Both these extremes express something of the truth about him, and it is tempting to suggest that they are merely two halves of the same coin, representing Hal in private and in public, respectively. But this is to miss the element of enigma in his portrayal. As with the question of Falstaff's cowardice, it is worth asking what it is that gives consistency to the evidence about Hal's character that has produced such conflicting views.

Hal is far from an open book to the other characters in the play. In *Part 2* the King is surely wrong in his weary sigh, 'Most subject is the fattest soil to weeds' (IV iv 54), and Warwick is nearer the truth when he urges that Hal is merely making use of Falstaff and his cronies. But Warwick too is wrong in the motive he imputes to the Prince: that he is acquainting himself with the baser side of life as part of a process of self-education in order to become the more perfect Christian governor later on. Critics have been more prone to use this defence of the Prince's conduct than Hal himself. He says nothing about it in his soliloquy in *Part 1*, 'I know you all' (I ii 188–210), discussed earlier (pp. 47–8). The most penetrating comment on this speech has been made by Dr

Johnson: it 'exhibits a natural picture of a great mind offering excuses to itself and palliating those follies which it can neither justify nor forsake'.[37] What Johnson has located here is the degree to which Hal is subject to conflicting pressures, being both attracted to Eastcheap and yet repelled by it. Equally important, Hal has little insight into his own motives. The explanation for his actions that he himself gives (to dazzle others later with his supposed reformation) is true enough at one level but is also a rationalisation and evasion.

In Act III of *Part 1* the King, in his interview with Hal, delivers a long speech accusing his son of being 'stale and cheap to vulgar company'. Evidently chastened by this rebuke, Hal replies – and there is nothing to suggest any insincerity – 'I shall hereafter, my thrice-gracious lord,/Be more myself' (III ii 92–3). But in the very next scene he is back in the Boar's Head, where his identification with the Eastcheap life appears to be unreserved; he refers to Falstaff with something like real affection as 'my sweet beef' (III iii 176), and the King's words to him in the previous scene find no echo in Hal's boast, 'I am good friends with my father, and may do anything' (ll. 180–1). It is in *Part 2* that Hal's disgust with the life he has been leading grows strongest. He directs a series of undisguised insults to Poins: 'What a disgrace is it to me to remember thy name . . .' (II ii, 12–13) Yet even at the end of this scene he cannot bring himself to decline Poins' suggestion that they don leather jerkins and aprons, and wait on Falstaff at his table. Hal in the event hardly enjoys his pantomime. The scene forms an instructive contrast with the gaiety and relative innocence of the scene parallel to it (II iv) in *Part 1*. Eventually he leaves with the perfunctory words 'Falstaff, good night' (II iv 354). They are the last words he speaks to Falstaff before the rejection.

Hal is neither introspective nor given to self-examination. He prefers to repress his inner conflicts and leave them to find their own resolution rather than allow them to well up into consciousness where they have to be confronted and dealt with. The method works. Neither his opening soliloquy nor anything he says later gives the impression of inner tension, of subjection to contradictory impulses which he cannot reconcile. His actions show that he feels now attraction, now disgust, but he seems unable to view both side by side in his mind at one time. They work out their own resolution, and it is never in doubt that the impulse to responsibility and respectability will prove the stronger. Hal progresses at the end of *Part 2* to some sort of maturity – that involved in the willing acceptance of his public role and duties – but without ever attaining the degree of self-knowledge that even Falstaff displays, and certainly without reaching any understanding of the impulses which drove him initially to embrace Falstaff and ultimately to reject him.

V

As a final point about the pervasiveness of ambiguity in the *Henry IV* plays, I want to look at how Shakespeare handles the ending of each part. The way in which he rounds off *Part 1* obviously bears on the much-debated question of whether they were conceived together or whether *Part 2* was a later addition capitalising on the success of the earlier play. I would argue for a compromise view. When Shakespeare wrote *Part 1* he was keeping his options open, and consequently the final effect of *Part 1* was intended to be slightly open-ended. On the one hand he had to make sure that the play had its own integrity. On the other (and here I am working back from the evidence of what he actually wrote) he wanted to leave a few loose ends. Not too many, of course, and not too obviously; but enough to create in the audience, subliminally perhaps, a sense that certain aspects of the play have not been fully dealt with, that they have within them the seeds of further development.

First there is the conclusion of the main external action of the play, the rebellion. On the face of it the battle of Shrewsbury is decisive. The rebels are defeated; Hotspur, who had given life and fire to the rebel cause, is dead; and the King is able to refer to what is left of the rebellion in terms of a mopping-up operation. And yet the fact that even this much is necessary is significant. Furthermore, the audience may have registered, subconsciously anyway, the import of Act IV scene iv, an unobtrusive pre-battle scene, in which the Archbishop of York and one Sir Michael discuss somewhat apprehensively the likely outcome. Fearful of Hotspur's defeat the Archbishop is sending letters to other allies to ensure that the defeated remnants of the battle (he seems to have remarkable prescience in this respect) can regroup and put up further resistance to the King: ''tis but wisdom to make strong against him' (l. 39). Here Shakespeare is dropping a clue to the audience (and a reminder to himself) that the rebellion is not over, and in so doing has prepared the ground for what will prove to be one of the main narrative strands in the sequel.

At the level of character relationships Shakespeare in *Part 1* also needs to bring to a head and resolve the all-too-obvious tension between Hal and his father. Shrewsbury forms the focus of this resolution. By his conduct in the battle he dispels his father's opinion that he has 'a truant been to chivalry' (v i 94): he kills Hotspur and saves Henry's life when he is threatened by Douglas, an act which elicits the King's commendation:

> Thou hast redeem'd thy lost opinion;
> And show'd thou mak'st some tender of my life,
> In this fair rescue thou hast brought to me.
>
> (v iv 48–50)

The sight of the King in danger of his life being rescued by his supposedly errant son forms a most compelling dramatic image; their mutual reconciliation could hardly be more fittingly achieved. But Hal's lack of the chivalric and martial virtues was not the only matter that earlier in the play had caused the King concern. In their interview in Act iii scene ii Henry, while stressing the unfavourable comparison of Hal and Hotspur, had also complained bitterly about his son's failure to assume his less glamorous princely responsibilities:

> Yet let me wonder, Harry,
> At thy affections, which do hold a wing
> Quite from the flight of all thy ancestors.
> Thy place in council thou hast rudely lost,
> Which by thy younger brother is supplied . . . .
>
> (iii ii 29–33)

One would not expect the King to raise these matters at the moment his life had been saved. But they remain as a potential source of unease, and will bulk even larger in his fears about Hal in *Part 2*, especially in the confrontation between them in Act iv scene v. In Hal's rescue of his father from Douglas a reconciliation is effected between them which is necessary for our sense of the completeness and integrity of *Part 1*. Nevertheless, without disrupting the genuineness of the reconciliation, Shakespeare has unobtrusively hinted at other aspects of their relationship, lightly contained within the framework of the whole, which are capable of being developed in a possible successor.

The third area which Shakespeare has to draw into focus at the end of *Part 1* is Hal's equivocal friendship with Falstaff. Hints have been dropped earlier with varying degrees of explicitness about Hal's attitude to his companion: his evasion in Act i scene ii of Falstaff's demands to know what will happen when he becomes king; his 'I know you all' soliloquy; and his response to Falstaff's half-serious appeal at the end of the play-scene in Act ii scene iv, 'Banish plump Jack, and banish all the world', of 'I do, I will' (ii iv 462–4). Such touches were designed to prevent the audience from sentimentalising the relationship between the two of them. It is also possible, though we cannot be sure, that they were intended as part of the long-term preparation for the overt rejection at the end of *Part 2*. Their presence is consistent with such a view, but they do not point unequivocally in that direction. In this area of the play, as in the others just mentioned, Shakespeare resolves his dramatic material in a way that is satisfying in itself while carrying the seeds of further development. He creates in *Part 1* a less extreme, symbolic rejection, which effectively defines the distance between Hal and Falstaff but without the finality that would prevent the continuation of the relationship in a possible sequel. The occasion is provided at the battle of Shrewsbury with the death of Hotspur. Hal turns from the corpse of his principal enemy to the supposed corpse of what in the play has been his greatest friend:

> What, old acquaintance! Could not all this flesh
> Keep in a little life? Poor Jack, farewell!
> I could have better spar'd a better man.
> O, I should have a heavy miss of thee,
> If I were much in love with vanity!
> Death hath not struck so fat a deer today,
> Though many dearer, in this bloody fray. (v iv 102–8)

The crucial lines are, 'I should have a heavy miss of thee,/If I were much in love with vanity!' The term 'vanity' has its own resonance, and, lightly done as it is, the speech defines, with some regretful affection, the heavily circumscribed limits on Hal's association with Falstaff.

Part 2 is far from being a tedious repetition of *Part 1*. Despite similarities of structure and the retention of many of the same characters, it is palpably a different play. The difference is felt immediately in its general tone: less high-spirited and buoyant, slower, bitter at times, suffused with a sense of disease, loss, the past, old age and death. The tonal difference is to some extent dictated by the direction

Shakespeare's material was taking in *Part 2*. It was moving towards a climax in the simultaneous apotheosis of Hal as the newly crowned Henry V and the final rejection of Falstaff. Whether or not this eventual conclusion was in Shakespeare's mind when he began *Part 1*, by the time he started *Part 2* he must have realised that such an ending was not going to be easy to achieve. Falstaff's known popularity on the Elizabethan stage suggests that he had outgrown the role allotted to him.

How then was his final expulsion to be effected without some risk of groans and whistles directed by the audience at the King who had just performed it? It was not merely the tradition of Henry V's virtuous reformation that made such a conclusion undesirable; the sound of Shakespeare's audience booing an English king (unless it were Richard III) would have attracted unwelcome official attention to the dramatist who had stimulated such *lèse-majesté*. The ways in which Shakespeare sets out to render Falstaff less attractive are well known. He seems more gross, less witty, and is burdened with age and disease. His way of life is more obviously squalid, and we, no less than the Prince, are meant to be repelled by it – and no doubt we are. Falstaff and Hal are kept physically apart much of the time, and Falstaff is moved from the centre of affairs in London to Gloucestershire and the company of the antique justices Shallow and Silence.

Shakespeare's skill in establishing a pervasive tone-colour for this play is such that Falstaff is made to seem an imaginative reflection of the world he inhabits: self-interested, devious, unprincipled – a world where the trick by which Prince John triumphs at Gaultree Forest recalls, in sad contrast, the chivalric idealism of Hal's offer in *Part 1* to decide the battle of Shrewsbury by meeting Hotspur in single combat. Shakespeare's unobtrusive art is sustained with a sure touch through the bulk of the play, and it is only towards the end that we start to detect the dramatist's hand manipulating his material towards the desired conclusion. As Clifford Leech has rightly noted, 'From the Prince's last interview with his father to the rejection of Falstaff, Shakespeare strives to make the morality-element all-pervading.'[38] The presentation of both Hal and Falstaff starts to take on more of a simple black-and-white character, with an inevitable loss of dramatic subtlety.

As evidence of a coarsening in the texture of the play there is the short melodramatic scene, Act v scene iv, in which Doll Tearsheet and Mistress Quickly are dragged off by the beadles. Doll may be a prostitute, but Mistress Quickly is hardly the professional bawd we are shown in *Pericles*. There are suggestions in the play that her personal fortunes have taken a turn for the worse; she had a husband in *Part 1* and refers to herself as a widow in *Part 2*; she tries, if with decreasing success, to maintain her 'reputation'. As a result this scene is pitched on a rather strident note, suggesting a Shakespeare over-anxious that we should react with appropriate revulsion. Plausibility is stretched to breaking-point when the first beadle says, 'the man is dead that you and Pistol beat amongst you' (p. 17–18); one blinks momentarily at the thought of Pistol actually beating anyone, of Mistress Quickly even allowing him on her premises ('there comes no swaggerers here' [II iv 76–7]), and still more of her actively abetting him.

The function of this scene is to show Falstaff's world in its worst aspect, the Elizabethan *demi-monde* of lust and anarchic violence ('There hath been a man or two lately kill'd about her' [v iv 6–7]). This is the reality of the Eastcheap life with which Falstaff is and Hal, by implication, has been associated. The belief that Hal was wholly given over to this world prompted the King's fear that, on his death, 'the fifth Harry from curb'd license plucks/The muzzle of restraint' (IV v 131–2). The substance of the fear rested only in the way we see Falstaff preparing to put into effect his threat that 'the laws of England are at my commandment' (v iii 135), and from his peak of illusory power Falstaff is at last dislodged. In the rejection speech the new King reinforces once again the view of Falstaff as 'The tutor and the feeder of my riots' (v v 63), and this condemnation, delivered with the full weight of regal authority, clearly represents the final view of Falstaff we are meant to carry with us at the end of the play.

Nevertheless, in trying to organise our sympathies away from Falstaff and gather them exclusively round Hal, Shakespeare is obliged to effect a considerable simplification. Not least in the version of his un-regenerate past which the King now offers to the world: he was an innocent, led astray, his 'riots' fed by Falstaff and 'the rest of my misleaders'. We are being asked to see Falstaff too and what he represents less clearly than we saw it in the past. He had exposed the absence of a dimension to Hal's vision of the world through his very willingness to laugh at himself; Hal's sense of humour had never extended to his own person, and Falstaff in his soliloquy on sherris in Act IV scene iv had shrewdly diagnosed its origins in the 'cold blood' of the Bolingbroke family. We are further being encouraged to put out of our minds our earlier awareness that Falstaff's self-interested opportunism had merely represented in unabashed form a spirit that pervaded the entire world of the play. We are now being asked to see Hal exclusively as the regenerate and duly constituted head of state purging both himself and the body politic of the forces of disorder and anarchy.

This seems to be Shakespeare's chosen framework; and yet, while working within it, he cannot rest content with this level of perceptiveness, however desirable it might be for the play's unity of effect. And so there is the ineluctable sense of pain which we feel on Falstaff's rejection and the complementary sense of the lack of humanity in the way it is carried out. These reactions are not the result of *our* greater awareness of the implications of what Shakespeare was doing, or of our superior humanity. They are the result of Shakespeare's own awareness and humanity, which would not let him settle for a perfection of form when it meant being untrue to that which the form enclosed. It is entirely characteristic of Shakespeare that in the very process of achieving a final resolution, he should give to Hal a speech ('I know thee not, old man. Fall to thy prayers' – v v 48–73), which undermines, however slightly, the structure it was designed to complete.

Shakespeare's problems with *Henry IV, Part 2* recall analogous problems that he had with *Love's Labour's Lost*. In each play he knew, in broad terms, what sort of ending he wanted, and in each case there is a slight but detectable forcing of the spontaneous energies of the drama in order to achieve it. Shakespeare has to convince us, almost against our better judgement, that the ladies in *Love's Labour's Lost* are superior in character and insight to the men, and that the men still have much to learn. In *Henry IV, Part 2* he has to gain our assent to a Falstaff whose appearance becomes progressively more tarnished and a Hal who is by contrast increasingly well scrubbed. Precisely because there is no similar perceivable effort in *Part 1*, because there is such ease and assurance in its complex unfolding, the earlier work is the supreme history play.

The most useful way into both parts of *Henry IV* remains that suggested by A. P. Rossiter. What they show us (to quote again) is 'realistic apprehension outrunning the medieval frame. Because the Tudor myth system of Order, Degree, etc. was too rigid, too black-and-white, too doctrinaire and narrowly moral for Shakespeare's mind.' The process described here – Shakespeare's provisional framework being qualified, altered, rendered ambiguous, as his imagination works within it – can be observed in other plays as well. Nevertheless, to return to the distinction made in the opening chapter, there is a difference between complexity and contradiction, between an artist's attempt to do justice to what is genuinely ambivalent in experience and his pursuit of what appear to be contrary and divergent artistic aims. *The Tempest*, I shall argue, is a play of this latter kind.

4 *The Tempest*

The Tempest has a special place in Shakespeare's work: not only his last complete play, but also his shortest; one of the handful he wrote which seem to obey the classical unities; one of the few for which there is no known literary source; and (the significance of this we can only guess at) given pride of place by Heminge and Condell at the front of the First Folio. For all the admiration it has received, it is not a play that one instinctively warms to. The enchanted island resists any easy identification with our own familiar world. The play's appeal lies both in the sense of wonder induced by its strangeness, its otherness, and, at a rather different level, in the fact that it has always been something of a challenge for critics. The play is an enigma, seeming both to contain Meaning, of a kind conceivably more significant than that of Shakespeare's previous plays, and yet refusing to disclose what that meaning is. *The Tempest* may not have produced the greatest amount of critical disagreement of all the plays; there are too many candidates vying for that particular honour. But it can probably lay claim to have inspired the greatest number of really daft interpretations.

Because of the play's enigmatic quality, criticism of *The Tempest* amounts to an even less coherent body of knowledge than criticism of Shakespeare's other plays. There seems to lurk a residual uncertainty about what kind of object it is, what kind of engagement with it is being invited, and what kind of approach is or is not going to prove fruitful. At the risk of some simplification, it is possible to see in *Tempest* criticism two ways of approaching the play which are quite distinct both emotionally and intellectually. One is determinedly no-nonsense, refusing to have the wool pulled over its eyes, insisting on seeing what is palpably there to be seen, and regarding the atmospheric penumbra of the play as a graceful irrelevance. This approach is the result of character criticism taken to extremes. The other is less concerned with surface effects, more willing – even insistent – to progress beyond mere

73

appearances to the hidden core of metaphysical significance. This approach leads to interpretations of the play in allegorical terms. Since *The Tempest* stimulates both approaches, it is worth looking at each in turn and then trying to see if both together reveal more about the play than either on its own.

I

In the opinion of E. E. Stoll the play 'is a story in its own right and for its own sake. . . . That the story is slight is no proof that there is another within or behind it.'[1] If that is the case, what we are presumably left with are the various characters and very little else. To expose the characters, Prospero in particular, to the harsh light of this conception of the play can be both startling and revealing:

> To an irreverent eye, the ex-Duke of Milan would perhaps appear as an unpleasantly crusty personage, in whom a twelve years' monopoly of the conversation had developed an inordinate propensity for talking. These may have been the sentiments of Ariel, safe at the Bermoothes; but to state them is to risk at least ten years in the knotty entrails of an oak, and it is sufficient to point out, that if Prospero is wise, he is also self-opinionated and sour, that his gravity is often another name for pedantic severity, and that there is no character in the play to whom, during some part of it, he is not studiously disagreeable.[2]

> Prospero . . . has a certain dryness; he does not impress the critical observer with quite the greatness he might be supposed to possess. His mysterious art is not allied with corresponding mysterious depths of his nature. On the contrary, he unintentionally appears in the light of a schoolmaster, constantly giving Ariel 'good marks', and, with an undertone of self-satisfaction, speaking perpetually and in a most consequential manner of his own capabilities and his own knowledge.[3]

This way of looking at Prospero is in varying degrees present in the writings of many critics of *The Tempest*. It was taken to its furthest limits in an essay by George Garrett with the sprightly title, 'That Four-Flusher Prospero'. He regards Prospero as vindictive, selfish and ruthless, concerned only with his own interests and the success of his project. 'He is a tyrant, a bully, a demon. He is chockful of vanity. Every move he makes is to show what he can do. Nobody can stop him.'⁴ The storm scene he considers an instance of Prospero's viciousness:

> 'There's no harm done', Prospero has twice told Miranda. If the scaring of helpless people to such an extent that they believe hell is let loose is no harm, what is? A thunder and lightning storm at sea is an act of fiendishness. 'In every cabin I flamed amazement'. Everybody on the ship must suffer accordingly. They do, or why would they 'plunge in the foaming brine'? The rest of the fleet, believing the king's ship lost, are bound sadly for Naples. What matter, so long as all this suits Prospero's purpose?⁵

Garrett is here committing the common fault of character criticism: treating dramatic characters as if they were people in real life. However terrifying a shipwreck may be in actuality, in this shipwreck Shakespeare is at pains not to emphasise the fear of those involved. In the first scene Antonio and Sebastian are snarling at the Boatswain rather than worrying about their own plight, and Gonzalo ends the scene on a note of philosophical resignation. The abuse of which much of the scene consists is bracing rather than disturbing, and from the audience's point of view it all forms an exciting start to the play. The exclusion of a sense of terror in the opening scene is deliberate. Whatever our final feelings about Prospero may be, Shakespeare does not want him damned at the outset as an unfeeling sadist.

Nevertheless, the critics quoted so far have responded strongly to a strain of harshness in Prospero that is undeniably there. What are we to make of it? How important an aspect is it of his character as a whole, and how significant is it in the total effect of the play?

One reason why it is difficult to answer these questions is that in certain respects Prospero is resistant to the methods of traditional character criticism. He is a remote figure, curiously opaque; and one source of his opacity lies in his dramatic idiom, which is inexpressive and hard to interpret. One interpretative crux was discussed in the opening chapter: what sort of forgiveness does Prospero offer Antonio at the end of the play? The idiom in which he speaks is (significantly) shared at times by those who are closest to him, Miranda and Ferdinand. So close is it that on one occasion a speech assigned to Miranda in the Folio was given by some of the play's early editors to Prospero. (Its bitter tone was

considered out of keeping with Miranda's gentle nature, but the cause
of editorial head-scratching is not clear. Caliban had tried to rape her.
What else was she supposed to feel towards him?)

> Abhorred slave,
> Which any print of goodness wilt not take,
> Being capable of all ill! I pitied thee,
> Took pains to make thee speak, taught thee each hour
> One thing or other. When thou didst not, savage,
> Know thy own meaning, but wouldst gabble like
> A thing most brutish, I endow'd thy purposes
> With words that made them known. But thy vile race,
> Though thou didst learn, had that in't which good natures
> Could not abide to be with; therefore wast thou
> Deservedly confin'd into this rock, who hadst
> Deserv'dst more than a prison.   (I ii 351–62)

If this speech is in any way problematic, it is not in its surface emotional
tone, because that is clear enough, but in its hint of other emotional
colourings which imply a quite different view of the speaker. The
dominant tone is one of moral outrage which in the circumstances
entirely draws our sympathy, and the reason it seems uncomplicated is
that the mode is so external, impersonal and distanced. We tend to hear
the speech less as that of an affronted person than as the abstract
principle of affront; hence its interchangeability between Prospero and
Miranda. The fact that the condemnation takes on this formal air
inhibits any inclination on our part to psychologise it or try to see
beyond it. And yet, on the other hand, an invitation to do just that is, or
seems to be, present. For those who want to hear it – and that would
probably include all the critics quoted so far – there is the echo of a
different tone in Miranda's speech: of uncomprehending repugnance
('savage . . . A thing most brutish . . . thy vile race'); of something
close to a nagging self-justification ('I pitied thee . . . I endow'd thy
purposes / With words . . . therefore wast thou / Deservedly confin'd');
and an uncomfortably priggish consciousness of her and her father's
virtue ('any print of goodness . . . good natures').

The nub of the problem is that these different tones of voice, once
heard, become impossible to ignore. If our hearing has thus become
more acute, as it were, we cannot by an effort of will make it less so. It
becomes difficult to give the speech the earlier routine assent in which

references to Prospero and Miranda's 'good natures' were accepted as simple statements of fact. The manner of speaking shared by Prospero, Miranda and Ferdinand, because it is so formal, distanced and psychologically opaque, is capable of expressing strong feelings but is ill suited to nuance or complexity. Such hints of a more critical attitude to them as are detectable are far from easy to integrate into our picture of a Prospero and a Miranda whom most of the time the play seems to want us to admire. The problem exists most of all in relation to Prospero. Because we cannot be sure how far such hints are really there, they can, paradoxically, assume disproportionate significance in the minds of those critics who, as we have seen, are disposed to put the worst possible construction upon everything Prospero says and does.

II

The resistance which Prospero, Miranda and Ferdinand put up to detailed psychological analysis leads, by a natural process, to the question of allegorical interpretation of *The Tempest*. Since the conscious formality in the way they are created holds us slightly at a distance, surely this is a sign that we should look above or beyond them for their true significance. Out of such speculation is the impulse towards allegory born. Allegory, it is generally accepted, is not Shakespeare's characteristic way of writing. But maybe this play is an exception: there has been no lack of voices in the past to insist that it is.

As a literary form allegory is far from simple, lacking precise limits in either critical theory or artistic practice. The main features of allegory I am assuming here are: that there should be a one-to-one correspondence between an individual character and that which he represents; that this correspondence is part of Shakespeare's conscious design and is consistently worked out through the play; and that the correspondences express a coherent interpretation of the play.

What may be not unfairly regarded as the lunatic fringe of allegorical interpretation are those which claim the meaning of *The Tempest* is not what the innocent reader or spectator takes it to be; it is something else, something esoteric and hidden, which requires special elucidation. In one of the many accounts of the play which identify Prospero with Shakespeare himself, Ariel becomes Shakespeare's imagination, craving liberty but kept in servitude, Miranda is the drama to which Shakespeare gave birth, Milan from which he is exiled becomes

Stratford, and the enchanted island is either the stage, London, or the world. In contrast, Prospero is Shakespeare, Miranda is his art, and Ferdinand is Fletcher, to whom Shakespeare married his art when they collaborated on *Henry VIII* and *The Two Noble Kinsmen*. In another version of the Prospero–Shakespeare identification Sycorax becomes the dark lady, Ariel Shakespeare's passion for her, and Caliban the friend who betrayed him. Different entirely is the view of Caliban, Sycorax and Ariel as representing water, cloud and lightning, and the tempest which brings them together is a prophetic vision of modern culture, based on natural science, with electricity playing the major part. As a variant on this Ariel represents electricity and Caliban raw matter. In a Darwinian view of the play Caliban represents prehistoric man or the missing link, the transition from anthropoid ape to primitive man, while Prospero represents mankind's highest perfection. *The Tempest* has also been seen as a prophetic vision of a different social order, in which Ariel represents active intelligence, Miranda art, and the marriage of Ferdinand and Miranda the penetration of art by morally purified force. The play has also been regarded as an allegorical history of the Christian Church, in which Prospero represents traditional Christianity, Miranda the Virgin Mary, Gonzalo conscience, and the tempest itself the Reformation.

Those are all nineteenth-century interpretations. In the present century it has been argued that *The Tempest* presents a myth of redemption through the rites of Eleusis, in which Prospero is God, Ariel is the Angel of the Lord, Caliban is the Devil, and Miranda is the Celestial Bride. Alternatively the play is a psychic allegory in which various characters represent aspects of Prospero's soul: Miranda the principle of Love, Gonzalo that of Fidelity, and Caliban the unregenerate aspect of himself. A different form of psychic allegory maintains that Prospero is the rational soul, Ariel is the sensitive soul, and Caliban the vegetative soul. Recently the suggestion has been put forward that the play is the covert expression of seventeenth-century Rosicrucianism, in which Prospero is Shakespeare's version of John Dee, the mathematician and astrologer in Queen Elizabeth's court.[6]

What strikes one about many of these interpretations is the simple difficulty of knowing how they could be proved either true or false. They are not so much interpretations of the text as reflections stimulated by it. The further from the text the wilder the speculation. If one makes the initial assumption – as some of the earlier commentators do – that the characters are in essence other than what they appear to be, there is literally no end to the ingenious flights of fancy which may then masquerade as criticism. It becomes a game we can all join in. Why may we not regard *The Tempest* as a concealed re-enactment of an episode in Shakespeare's past? Caliban (not Prospero) is Shakespeare; he has after all some of the best poetry in the play. Prospero is John Shakespeare, who nevertheless refuses to recognise Caliban – William as his son until the end of the play, and very reluctantly even then. The cause of their estrangement was the unsuitable match enforced on Shakespeare when he got Anne Hathaway pregnant. The marriage of Ferdinand and Miranda is an allegorical vision of the ideal marriage which Shakespeare senior had hoped his son would make but which had demonstrably failed to come about in practice; please note Prospero – John Shakespeare's constant harping on the importance of pre-marital chastity.

This hypothesis, for all its absurdity, is not different in kind from the ones just referred to. In fact I am not sure it isn't better than some of them. But there are two principles which can act as a curb on allegorical interpretations, especially on the more inventive ones. First, they should not be arbitrary. We should feel a genuine, unforced imaginative connection between the character and that of which he is said to be the allegorical expression. Secondly, whatever the character signifies allegorically, he also remains what we directly perceive him to be, a character involved in a dramatic action. With these principles in mind we can now consider one of the most popular ways in which Prospero has been allegorised. Although occasionally regarded as Providence or Destiny, he has been more often taken, with greater or lesser confidence, to be the allegorical representation of God.

The deification of Prospero goes back, like most allegorical interpretations, to the nineteenth century. No doubt this claim, with its accompanying requirement to feel a proper degree of awe and reverence for Prospero himself, helped to set off the irritated counter-reaction of Garrett and the others mentioned earlier. But it has survived despite their attentions. Wilson Knight described Prospero as 'a close replica of Christ',[7] and F. D. Hoeniger claims that 'Shakespeare endows him with the power of those divine forces which . . . from time to time interfere in human affairs.'[8] C. J. Sisson sees Prospero as 'the Vicar of God in his own country, a visible Providence'.[9] The most recent study in this vein, by Thomas McFarland, claims that 'the goodness that flows from Prospero, in his island haven, represents not only absolute benignity but absolute power as well', Prospero being 'the anthropomorphic figure of the divine'.[10]

With the possible exception of McFarland, none of these writers is prepared to say in so many words that Prospero *is* God, although they all come close to it. But even going as far as they do may be going too far. One recollects not only Prospero's un-Godlike attributes of testiness and impatience so enthusiastically marshalled by Garrett and the others, but also the fact that Prospero at key points in the play illustrates unequivocally his limited and finite nature. He forgets things; the masque that he puts on for Ferdinand and Miranda in Act IV dominates his attention to the exclusion of Caliban's conspiracy. And at the very beginning of the play he makes clear how circumscribed is his power:

> By accident most strange, bountiful Fortune,
> Now my dear lady, hath mine enemies
> Brought to this shore; and by my prescience
> I find my zenith doth depend upon
> A most auspicious star, whose influence
> If now I court not, but omit, my fortunes
> Will ever after droop.   (I ii 178–84)

Prospero acknowledges that he is subservient to both time and Fortune, and this is an impression of him we are presumably meant to carry with us into the play.

And yet this somehow fails to say it all. The instinct to see in Prospero more than just a man is not baseless. We have already noticed the curious impersonality of his speech patterns. The deifiers of Prospero can point to the fact that on the island at least he has absolute power, that he can control the destinies of all the people on it, and that he seems to be using his power for benign ends. There is in addition the absence of close personal contact with any character in the play except Miranda, together with the fact that his relations with everyone, even Miranda, are largely instrumental and indirect. While these may be curious and perhaps unattractive features if we view Prospero as a man, they also have a cumulative power to transfigure our awareness of him – not enough necessarily to convince us that he is God, but enough to instil in us a troubled awe.

The conclusion to which this discussion of allegory is leading is that it is altogether too blunt an instrument to be of very much help in elucidating the play. *The Tempest* contains within itself the impulse towards unambiguous simplicity and clarity of outline – towards the explicit correspondences of allegory in fact – while at the same time constantly thwarting and subverting any over-confident moves in that direction.[11]

III

No less than its central character, the entire world of *The Tempest* is enigmatic and difficult to grasp. Because it is enigmatic, it is for that very reason remarkably suggestive.

This quality of the play has been admirably described by Anne Barton:

> *The Tempest* is an extraordinarily obliging work of art. It will lend itself to almost any interpretation, any set of meanings imposed upon it: it will even make them shine. The danger of this flexibility, this capacity to illustrate arguments and systems of thought outside itself, is that it can lead critics to mistake what is really their own adaptation for the play. To talk about *The Tempest*, even to try to describe it, without adding to it in terms of motivation, psychology, themes, or ideas, is extremely difficult. As with one of the seminal myths of the classical world, all interpretation beyond a simple outline of the order of events, a list of the people taking part, runs the risk of being incremental. Criticism of this play is often illuminating in itself, as a structure of ideas, without shedding much light on its ostensible subject. It may falsely limit Shakespeare's achievement. Troubling, complex, exasperating, the original is infinitely greater and more suggestive than anything that can be made out of it.[12]

What Dr Barton is saying here seems to me an insight of fundamental significance, as important for criticism of *The Tempest* as Rossiter's 'Ambivalence: the Dialectic of the Histories' was for criticism of the *Henry IV* plays. It explains both the proliferation of allegorical criticism in the past and why so much of it has been misdirected. It also goes some way to accounting for the divergent responses to Prospero.

At this point it is as well to draw attention to such critical consensus as exists concerning *The Tempest*. A useful point of reference has been the group of plays to which it seems to belong, the last romances, which, despite differences in structure, have themes, preoccupations and motifs in common. Viewed in that context what is most evident about *The Tempest* is that it enacts a movement from disharmony to harmony, that it deals with sinfulness past and present, and that the conclusion is characterised by repentance, forgiveness and reconciliation. There is a central tradition in *Tempest* criticism which either acknowledges or directly concerns itself with this process. A representative example is Derek Traversi's discussion of the play:

> As in *The Winter's Tale*, the storm and the calm which follows it are related respectively to the tragedy caused by human passion and the reconciliation which, after a period of trial to which the actors are exposed in order to determine their respective responsibilities and access to redemption, follows upon repentance in its aftermath. . . . Prospero emerges increasingly, as the plot takes shape, as the instrument of judgement. Through his actions, and those of Ariel acting at his behest, the different motives which prevail in his former enemies are brought to the surface, evaluated and finally judged. In the process of judgement, the meeting of Prospero's daughter with the son of Alonso provides a symbolic ground for reconciliation in the familiar Shakespearean manner. Only after the final restoration of harmony, and the judgement that precedes it, have taken place on the island does Prospero, with his restored associates, return to resume his place in the human society from which envy and ambition had originally driven him.[13]

Traversi makes much of the moment in Act III when Ariel removes the enchanted banquet from Alonso and his companions, referring particularly to Ariel's address to them, 'You are three men of sin' (III iii 53–82), with its final admonition about the necessity of 'heart's sorrow / and a clear life ensuing'. 'Here at last –', Traversi comments, 'rather even than in any speech so far spoken by Prospero – is an explicit statement of what *The Tempest* is about.'[14]

The general thrust of this account, if not all the details, would probably command a cautious assent from most people – the play dramatises a process of moral purgation leading eventually to peace and reconciliation. But, even if one grants that this is the play's controlling structure, what one wants to know is *why* Shakespeare chose to dramatise this process in the manner summed up by Dr Barton – a manner so elusive that (to take only two examples) it is far from clear to what extent Prospero himself is required to participate in this regenerative process, as opposed to merely directing it from the outside, and also how successful the process is finally meant to be, how confidently affirmative the play's conclusion.

My belief is that Shakespeare wrote it in this way because of the inherent contradictions in his chosen material. The peculiar reticence of the play, its reluctance to declare itself, represent the dramatist's attempt to deal with deep internal divisions. *The Tempest* demonstrates, in an unusually acute form, the conflict present in varying degrees in those plays we have looked at so far: that is, between the conscious demands of art, of formal pattern-making, and that larger human awareness which resists imaginative shaping. Formal allegory may have been on the whole an uncongenial form for Shakespeare, perhaps because it involved a movement away from the level of instinctual and accumulated experience where his creative roots lay. Nevertheless, there are signs in this play that Shakespeare seems to have wanted to shape his subject-matter into something like allegory, while at the same time subverting that tendency by developing and exploring his material in an altogether freer and less constricted way. His unresolved intentions led to the distinctive qualities of *The Tempest* – brevity, inexplicitness, impenetrability.

With one part of himself, to judge from intermittent evidence in the play, Shakespeare seems to want to offer Prospero, Miranda and Ferdinand to us as images of regenerated humanity purged of its baser instincts. Prospero is, at this level, a representative of divine justice, powerful, wise, beneficent (Shakespeare's success at carrying out this part of his intention is illustrated by those critics who regard Prospero as a God-figure), and Miranda – and by extension Ferdinand too – are products of uncorrupted nature and Prospero's nurture. Ferdinand reinforces this exalted view by referring to Miranda as 'So perfect and so peerless' (iii i 47) and by his exclamation,

> Let me live here ever;
> So rare a wond'red father and a wise
> Makes this place Paradise. (iv i 122–4)

The words do more than express his love of Miranda and respect for his future father-in-law. They also point to Shakespeare's intention of creating images of redeemed humanity and, in the case of Miranda and Ferdinand, of a perfected man–woman relationship. 'Let me live here ever' and 'Paradise' even carry suggestions of a prelapsarian Adam and

Eve in the Garden of Eden. Such a conception of Miranda and Ferdinand is bound to be formal and idealised, and it is entirely appropriate that their betrothal should be celebrated in that most formal and artificial of structures, the masque that dominates Act IV. The projection of goodness and virtue on to the figures of Prospero, Miranda and Ferdinand inevitably requires its opposite to be projected on to Caliban and the three Neapolitan sinners, Antonio, Sebastian and Alonso.

Shakespeare's problem here was compounded by his use of the romance form. Some years ago Frank Kermode wrote that 'there is still much to be *known* about the romances'.[15] As a small contribution to the ensuing debate I would merely question its appropriateness for Shakespeare's purposes in this play. In *The Tempest* he is trying to use the romance form to express something about human nature, not merely as embodied on the island, but as it exists in that larger, more complicated world which romance excludes; and gradually, it seems to me, he came to doubt the validity of anything built on such foundations. At all events – this perhaps puts my objection more sharply – romance is an intrinsically unsuitable form for the kind of play Shakespeare wanted to write, a drama of psychological change and of spiritual and moral transformation.

IV

Shakespeare's unresolved dramatic intentions are detectable in the way he portrays some of his characters. Ferdinand's origins in the world of romance are obvious enough. His character rests on the entirely conventional assumption that virtue associated with noble birth is both innate and incapable of being sullied. The fact that his father conspired with Antonio to replace Prospero as Duke of Milan; the fact that, if Alonso and Sebastian set its tone, the court of Naples must have been a place of intrigue and corruption – all this seems to have affected Ferdinand not one whit. As a result Prospero's testing of him in the log-bearing episode is entirely gratuitous. What is the point of thus inculcating the virtues of self-control and self-discipline in someone who shows no signs of lacking them? (Drawing his sword earlier at Prospero's threat to manacle his feet and neck together scarcely indicated lack of self-control – merely a quite proper instinct for self-preservation.) Carrying logs has no obviously improving effect on his character. How could it, when there was so little space for improvement to start with?

Shakespeare's problem is that he wants to regard Ferdinand as simultaneously belonging and not belonging to that world outside the island where human nature is an unequal blend of good and bad, where an individual's character is not in a state of preternatural fixity, and where change is often desirable and sometimes even possible. This dual conception of Ferdinand lies behind the awkwardness we feel later at Prospero's repeated warnings to him not to make love to Miranda until they are married. The warnings, excessive by any standards, are peculiarly inappropriate to Ferdinand. He is more than a proper young man. He is the very nonpareil of propriety, whose feelings towards Miranda, expressed in language of a formality which constantly verges on the sententious, seem confined to the worshipful and adoring. Prospero's strictures belong to the world of unregenerated humanity – to Caliban, say, whose sexuality is as rampant as Ferdinand's is dormant – and Shakespeare is quite unable to make them seem imaginatively relevant to the Ferdinand we are shown.

Miranda is more fully sketched in than Ferdinand, but she too is as much a representative or symbolic figure as an individual one. She has been regarded as 'a paradisal figure untainted by human sin'.[16] Less exaltedly perhaps, the significance of Miranda and her future husband has been expressed in these terms: 'of Ferdinand and Miranda we shall say, if I may risk allegorising them, that they represent the hope by which we live and without which we could not bear the burden of our lives'.[17] So indeed they may have done for Shakespeare as well; but not without reservations.

Shakespeare was unable to offer them for our unqualified admiration, partly because they were so limited, more because they were too abstracted from the humanity they were meant to grace to be wholly convincing. They lack the vitality and capacity for intense experience of Florizel and Perdita in *The Winter's Tale*. They seem the product of an excessively pondered desire on Shakespeare's part for explicit Significance. There is something thin, attenuated, even insubstantial about them, and as a result they are threatened by the creeping blight of unreality, the dissolution of substance into shadow, which is given most memorable expression in Prospero's speech 'Our revels now are ended' (IV i 147–58). The symbolic hope that they represent is precious, but one wonders whether they are strong enough to bear it. Shakespeare's doubts about the strength of the positive ideal they embody, in particular about Miranda's innocent vulnerability, are expressed through Prospero's reply to her joyful exclamation at the end of the play:

> How many goodly creatures are there here!
> How beauteous mankind is! O brave new world
> That has such people in't!   (v i 182–4)

Prospero's sadly ironic reply, ''Tis new to thee', made in fuller knowledge of the men she is marvelling at, points forward to a world of experience of which she knows nothing. Miranda, product of innocent nature and her father's nurture, must return to the world from which she came, and Shakespeare, through Prospero, cannot repress a tremor about how she will fare.

Caliban complements the civilised virtue of Ferdinand and Miranda in his embodiment of primitive appetite and aggressiveness. At one level the conception of Caliban can be taken to be as simple in its own way as that of Ferdinand and Miranda; he lumbers through Act I, growling hatred and defiance of Prospero, and remains 'this thing of darkness' (v i 275) even at the end. If we can equate Prospero with God, surely we can equate Caliban with the Devil. The relevant quotation lies ready to hand: Prospero's judgement on him, 'A devil, a born devil, on whose nature / Nurture will never stick' (iv i 188–9). Tempting though it may be, such an identification is scarcely possible. Despite his origins as the offspring of a devil, which presumably explain his lust and murderousness, he is a remarkable mixture. If he is vindictive and abusive, he also shows a surprising desire and ready gratitude for human comfort and affection; despite a strong will to freedom he is remarkably disposed to subordinate himself to others and to obey them; and, although a creature of sensual appetites, he also has a primitive religious sense and the instinct to worship, as well as an imaginative capacity for dreaming and responding to music.

Caliban both is and is not susceptible to that moral improvement which Ferdinand both does and does not need. In Caliban's case one's view of the matter can be buttressed by whichever of two quotations one chooses to emphasise. On the one hand, as noted already, he is 'a born devil, on whose nature / Nurture will never stick'. On the other he is capable of saying (and presumably meaning?) 'I'll be wise hereafter / And seek for grace' (v i 294–5). It is difficult not to feel throughout the play a more or less continuous pressure on us to see Caliban as Prospero does, as a mere object of moral repugnance. But, like Falstaff, Caliban both invites and in some measure eludes simple moral condemnation. Although Falstaff and Caliban have been subjected by critics to reductive analysis – often in terms of their alleged literary antecedents – they remain powerfully original creations. Caliban has a more rich and interesting inner life than the other characters in *The Tempest*, and he seems to proceed from a deeper imaginative level than any other apart from Prospero himself.[18] The contradictions in his make-up reflect something of the unresolved conflicts in Shakespeare's attitude to his subject-matter as a whole.

The other main representative of depraved humanity, Antonio, does not have the same resonance – certainly none of the ambiguity. He is a familiar Shakespearean type, like Edmund in *King Lear* or even Richard III: the Machiavellian manipulator, the 'realist' overtaken eventually by a realism outside his calculations. If Prospero, Miranda and Ferdinand seem in many ways figures from the world of romance, Antonio – cynical, amoral, on the make – is evidently a visitor from a more familiar world. The racy vitality of his speech forms a sharp contrast to Miranda's words to Caliban discussed earlier. Here Antonio is trying to persuade Sebastian to kill Alonso and make himself King of Naples. Sebastian's half-hearted 'But, for your conscience –' is brushed aside with

> Ay, sir; where lies that? If 'twere a kibe,
> 'Twould put me to my slipper; but I feel not
> This deity in my bosom; twenty consciences
> That stand 'twixt me and Milan, candied be they,
> And melt, ere they molest! Here lies your brother,
> No better than the earth he lies, upon,
> If he were that which now he's like – that's dead;
> Whom I with this obedient steel, three inches of it,
> Can lay to bed for ever; whiles you, doing thus,
> To the perpetual wink for aye might put
> This ancient morsel, this Sir Prudence, who
> Should not upbraid our course. For all the rest
> They'll take suggestion as a cat laps milk;
> They'll tell the clock to any business that
> We say befits the hour.   (II i 267–81)

The construction of this speech is altogether freer and more flexible than Miranda's; the syntax is more daring (as in the sentence, 'twenty consciences . . . ere they molest'), the rhythms more lively; and there is a greater reliance on imagery of a vivid and energetic kind ('this ancient morsel, this Sir Prudence'). The sense of an individual mind in movement is infinitely greater than in the Miranda passage. Where Miranda merely addresses Caliban, Antonio is constantly persuading, cajoling, and inciting Sebastian in the desired direction.

There is a symbolic appropriateness in the fact that Antonio and Sebastian, unlike the other members of the court party, do not succumb to Ariel's spell in Act II scene i and fall asleep. This wide-awake quality in Antonio makes him a subtle threat to the whole dramatic world Shakespeare has created. It is an incitement to us to a similar resistance. Possibly for this reason Antonio is not developed very fully; after this scene, which ends with his and Sebastian's abortive attempt on the lives of Alonso and Gonzalo, he has only a dozen lines in the rest of the play. The effect of Antonio's alert cynical intelligence (manifested in his dissection of the logical flaws in Gonzalo's 'commonwealth' speech – ll. 141–63) is not something Shakespeare wants too much of in the play. The island is a world of magic, and its spell cannot work if met with too disenchanted or unblinking a gaze.

Critics nevertheless tend to divide into those who submit unresistingly to the enchantment of the whole and those who narrow their eyes and try to ensure that no ignorant fumes mantle their clearer reason. The former approach produces the more favourable view of Prospero himself. While we sit in wonder at Prospero's magic, we are not disposed to question or judge him. It is precisely this open-mouthed willingness to take Prospero on his own terms that provoked the irritable over-reaction of critics such as Garrett. Their insistence on Prospero's anger, vindictiveness, self-importance and so on has the cynical clarity, and perhaps also the limitations, of Antonio's own vision. The real question is how far the island magic is meant to work on us as well as on the various characters exposed to it on stage.

Ariel's address to Alonso and the others, 'You are three men of sin' (III iii 53–82), illustrates the problem. Ariel's sudden descent, the removal of the banquet, his words of condemnation invoking 'Destiny', 'Fate', 'the pow'rs', the presence of Prospero 'on the top, invisible' – all this amounts to more than a striking theatrical effect. The physical relationship of the characters on stage as well as what is spoken create the strongest impression so far that Prospero's magic power is symbolic of the divine. But with a certain conscious effort we can remind ourselves that Ariel and his fellow-spirits are *not* 'ministers of Fate', they are servants of Prospero; that Alonso has not been bereft of his son; and that the whole thing is a performance scripted, directed and applauded by Prospero himself ('Of my instruction hast thou nothing bated/In what thou hadst to say' – ll. 87–8). To the extent that we submit to the pressure to take Ariel's words unreflectingly, the speech forms part of a regressive strain in the play towards comforting, graspable moral certainties, towards, in particular, Prospero-as-God, all-powerful and all-wise. But the success of conjuring tricks, let alone of magic, is that we do not see how it is done. And in this case we do; Prospero is present throughout. We have to decide whether to respond to him as (to take the two extremes) a conjuror manipulating a stage audience though not us or a figure embodying the invisible processes of divine judgement.

V

At this stage it may be useful to look at *The Tempest* from the point of view of Prospero and the specific problems he poses. Broadly speaking, I am claiming the presence of two Prosperos in the play. One is wise and just, treated with all proper love and respect by Miranda and Ferdinand, a benevolent magician who, even in experiencing a second time the anger he felt at his brother's treachery, will nevertheless ultimately guide his enemies through purgatorial suffering to penitence, forgiveness and reconciliation. The other is complacent of his virtues, emotionally self-enclosed, unfeeling of the suffering he causes to the innocent Gonzalo, harsh to Ferdinand, unjust to Caliban, unjust even to Ariel, unstable and subject to rage, bent more on revenge than forgiveness, and capable at the end of only a grudging reconciliation with his brother. It is impossible to know how Shakespeare visualised Prospero at the outset, and on the evidence of what we have it seems likely he had not made up his mind. The degree of prominence in the play of the idealised Prospero is shown by all the Prospero-as-(symbolic)-God interpretations. But Shakespeare seems to have found a flawless Prospero either insufficiently interesting or too abstract to be plausible. So, without actually relinquishing the Platonic form of Prospero altogether, Shakespeare in practice is more taken up with dramatising a Prospero belonging to a world which exercised a stronger gravitational pull on his imagination, the sublunary world of imperfect humanity. And here there is a much more searching portrayal of

Prospero in his various roles of father, schoolmaster, ruler, even theatrical producer.

The idealised conception of the character nevertheless exerts an awkward counter-pull to all the other complex impressions that the play provides. Since the two Prosperos are incapable of being harmonised or reconciled, Shakespeare's task was to minimise the consequences of his indecision. His solution was the one noted earlier by Dr Barton: reticence and inexplicitness. Shakespeare's skill in this respect is such that certain points in the play are sufficiently opaque for them to be regarded, legitimately, as consistent with either reading of Prospero's character.

A simple example of what I mean is the question of whether Prospero was wrong – and whether he acknowledges he was wrong – in his fateful decision to cast the governorship of Milan onto his brother. If Prospero is as near perfect as he has been taken to be, the answer to both questions is 'No'. But several critics believe he was at fault, and that he comes to recognise the fact. 'In Prospero's description of the Milanese *coup d'état*, his passion for the contemplative life amounts to nothing less than a hedonist idyll – "my library / Was dukedom large enough" (II ii 109–10) – an escape from the public responsibilities of office into a private and insular world of art.'[19] An even stronger view: 'The Prospero we see at the beginning of *The Tempest* has already learned from the mistakes of his past that the misfortunes we attribute to chance are often of our making.'[20] Has he though? Here is what Prospero actually says:

> I thus neglecting worldly ends, all dedicated
> To closeness and the bettering of my mind
> With that which, but by being so retir'd,
> O'er-priz'd all popular rate, in my false brother
> Awak'd an evil nature; and my trust,
> Like a good parent, did beget of him
> A falsehood, in its contrary as great
> As my trust was.   (I ii 89–96)

The first words, 'I thus neglecting worldly ends', can be taken either as acknowledgement of error or as a proud assertion of his dedication to a higher ideal. The feeling in the rest of the passage, although strong, forcing its way through the labyrinthine syntax, fails to come into sharp focus. Prospero points to the connection between his action and

Antonio's treachery, but it is not clear where he is allocating blame. Although 'Awak'd' suggests an acknowledgement of personal responsibility for what happened, it has in its context an oddly neutral ring. Furthermore the difficulty in mentally connecting subject and main verb over five lines ('I . . . in my false brother/Awak'd an evil nature') almost creates the effect of anacoluthon, suggesting that the evil side of Antonio 'Awak'd' spontaneously. The comparison of his trust of Antonio to that of 'a good parent' is the most overt hint that Prospero is not blaming himself for what happened. The phrase I imagine invites a nod of approval from someone disposed to take Prospero on his own terms. On the other hand, from someone who is not it invites the rejoinder that a good parent is not one who says, 'Don't bother me, I'm busy', and then refuses to accept any responsibility for what mischief the child gets up to. So the evidence is inconclusive. It is in a form which enables us to believe whatever we want to believe.

What concerns Prospero most is not the past but the present, and the common motive behind all his actions in the play is his desire to control the action and destinies of everyone on the island. *The Tempest* is centrally concerned with the exercise of power over other people, power to do good and power to do harm, power rightfully used and power wrongfully used. These matters, most sharply focused in Prospero himself, determine the structure and organisation of the whole play. Or, to rephrase that more accurately, they determine the presentation of both Prosperos and the plays in which each one figures. For convenience I now call them the A and the B versions, since the logic of my argument requires me to make a schematic division within this unusually complex and difficult work.

In the A version Prospero exemplifies the rightful use of power. He is a supremely wise, benevolent magician exercising superhuman powers for the benefit of all, preventing the evil characters from committing harm, punishing them where necessary, and bringing them by slow degrees through suffering to repentance. The use of his powers both for control and moral improvement is not called in question. The function of Caliban and Ariel is to serve his purposes. His harshness to Caliban is necessary if the servant–monster, 'Whom stripes may move, not kindness' (I ii 345), is to be controlled. Ariel, grateful at being released from the cloven pine, is generally willing to do his master's bidding, and there is some affection between them ('Do you love me, master? No?' 'Dearly, my delicate Ariel' – IV i 48–9). Prospero's fatherly control over Miranda is part of his disinterested, loving concern for her happiness ('I

have done nothing but in care of thee' – I ii 16). The imposition of the
log-bearing on the virtuous Ferdinand is done to establish that he is a fit
husband for her. All the other examples in the play of the attempted
exercise of power represent, in contrast, its use for evil purposes.
Antonio's usurpation of Prospero's dukedom was a crime. The sub-plot
with Stephano and Trinculo's conspiracy to depose Prospero and make
Stephano king of the island is a comic re-enactment of the original
offence, and in a similar way Antonio and Sebastian's attempt on the
lives of Alonso and Gonzalo forms the second conspiracy which
Prospero has to forestall. Within this broad framework the play is one
where evil schemes are thwarted, the sinners are brought to a state of
'heart's sorrow, / And a clear life ensuing (III iii 81–2), and having
accomplished his mission Prospero finally relinquishes his magic art and
prepares to return to Milan. The play's happy ending is complete.

   The Tempest, on this selective reading, does not look very interesting.
Nor, one suspects, would it have looked very interesting to Shakespeare,
had it at any stage taken this precise form in his mind – and I am not
suggesting that it did, even though all the elements just described are
there in the play as finally written. The contrast between the good and
the bad characters is too stark, and Prospero, Miranda and Ferdinand,
whose virtues are being celebrated, offer too little stimulus to
Shakespeare's imagination. But, if the framework of the play is
unsatisfactory as it stands, it has potential; particularly in the contrast of
Prospero's eventual relinquishment of his magic art with his prior
exercise of absolute power on the island – and also in the complementary need of the various characters, human and non-human, for
freedom from his control. Then there is the question of the moral
justification of Prospero's absolute power; not to mention that of its
practical effectiveness: can his power not only affect actions but also
transform attitudes and feelings? And, apart from its effectiveness on
others, what about the effect of unlimited power on the man who wields
it?

   Exploration of such matters serves to remove the play and its
protagonist further from the realm of abstractions and brings both into
closer touch with the larger world of imperfect humanity. In the process
Prospero becomes a less purely admirable but much more compelling
dramatic creation.

   The B version of *The Tempest* directs us to the play's treatment of all
these questions. To begin with it suggests a new perspective on
Prospero's desire to control all the characters. It is no longer enough to

say that he is doing it for their own good. There is a hint of something obsessive about his urge to dominate. His insistence now on total control suggests indeed an over-reaction to his earlier failure to exercise any control at all over his dukedom. Furthermore, it is possible to see how Prospero's granting of freedom to all the other characters is something he is able to do only with great difficulty and even reluctance.

The first, and greatest, sacrifice he has to make is to relinquish his parental claim on Miranda. There is an uncharacteristic vulnerability in his exclamation in Act IV, 'O Ferdinand! / Do not smile at me that I boast her off' (IV i 8–9). In order to arrive at this point he has had to overcome an element of jealous possessiveness, evident in his anger both at her when she pleads for Ferdinand ('What, I say, / My foot my tutor?' – I ii 468–9) and at Ferdinand himself. The way he addresses the young man is curious. At their first meeting he twice calls him 'traitor' and adds 'thy conscience / Is so possess'd with guilt' (ll. 470–1). The language suggests an unconscious throwback to Antonio's treachery: Ferdinand has come to rob him of his dearest possession, Miranda, just as his treacherous brother had earlier robbed him of his dukedom. Later, when Ferdinand's trial is over and the need for even an acted show of anger is past, Prospero's first words to him in Act IV scene i are, 'If I have too austerely punish'd you . . . .' Why 'punish'd'? – unless Prospero is still projecting onto the guiltless Ferdinand the anger he feels at his brother.

Even at this stage Prospero is so far from foregoing total control over the young couple that he twice warns them of the importance of pre-marital chastity. This repeated insistence struck Clifford Leech as sufficiently excessive to require explanation not even in terms of Prospero's psychology but in terms of Shakespeare's: *The Tempest* is taken to be the final expression of the puritan impulse in Shakespeare himself, a horrified recoil from the sins of the flesh; and the sexual impluse, embodied in its most anarchic form in Caliban, is now viewed as a source of moral peril.[21] This may seem an extreme view. That it is not the only possible interpretation is pointed out by David William, writing in the spirit of the A version of the play:

> The puritanism of *The Tempest* is similar to that of *Comus*. That is to say, it is both positive and idealistic. . . . Prospero's sacramental attitude to sex can be presented as a thing of joy and love rather than as the restrictive suspiciousness of a prurient voyeur.[22]

'. . . a prurient voyeur' refers to the fact that Prospero is a hidden bystander throughout Ferdinand and Miranda's courtship. However little his right to be there is questioned in the A version (he is merely demonstrating his fatherly concern), it is impossible to believe that Shakespeare did not feel its indelicacy. William Empson referred scathingly to one of his asides ('Fair encounter / Of two most rare affections! Heavens rain grace / On that which breeds between 'em!' – III i 74–6) as 'the peeping and lip-smacking of the old goat Prospero'.[23] That too may be over-stated; but it holds an awkward truth.

Prospero's exercise of power in the A version is *de jure*; in the B version it is less *de jure* than *de facto*, a change which is reflected in Prospero's relations with his servants, Ariel and Caliban. His authority over them is less a matter of right than of competing wills, in which his need for their services involves the repression of their desire for freedom. Coercion in the form of threats and punishment is the only way Prospero can compel obedience in Caliban, whose cry 'This island's mine' (I ii 331) makes a powerful appeal to natural justice. The strength of his urge to be free (even as he lays fresh fetters on himself) comes out most strongly in the drunken chant that climaxes his first meeting with Stephano and Trinculo: 'Freedom, high-day! high-day, freedom! freedom, high-day, freedom!' (II ii 175–6). Ariel's servitude is less painfully borne because less unwillingly offered. On his side the residue of gratitude at being released from the cloven pine and on Prospero's some genuine if intermittent affection almost transform the master–servant relationship. But he and Prospero scarcely meet without Ariel's reminder that the time has nearly come for his deliverance. His indispensability to Prospero's purposes combined with his own yearning to shake off the other's yoke create a tension in Prospero that manifests as anger at times scarcely less violent and bitter in tone than that directed at Caliban. Of no creature in *The Tempest* than Ariel is it truer to say that liberty is his natural condition; but he is the last to receive it, and at the end he makes no response to Prospero's wistfully affectionate, 'My Ariel, chick' (v iii 316), as he receives his final charge.

Shakespeare's dramatisation of Prospero's use of his power is at its most complex and ambiguous in the matter of what the ex-Duke of Milan is proposing to do with his old enemies. According to the A version he intends from the outset to work towards harmony, reconciliation and forgiveness through submitting the sinners to a process of purgatorial suffering. The trouble with this conception of both protagonist and play is that it is undramatic. If Prospero is all-good as well as all-powerful, resistance to him is no less unjustifiable than it is futile; *The Tempest* will make its way to an all-too-predictable conclusion. The play, in short, lacks conflict. One way of remedying this omission is to internalise conflict within Prospero himself, and Shakespeare therefore creates a Prospero experiencing once again the anger he felt at his brother's treachery.

The presence of this anger is acknowledged by some of the critics in the A version, but not its power to alter Prospero's benign purposes. As Middleton Murry put it,

> The Island is a realm where God is Good, where true Reason rules; it is what would be if Humanity – the best in man – controlled the life of man. And Prospero is a man in whom the best in man has won the victory: not without a struggle, of which we witness the reverberation.[24]

There is a fine line dividing this conception of Prospero from those belonging in what, for convenience, I am calling the B version of the play. The more we register the disruptive power of Prospero's anger, the more we question the inevitability of the play's ending in peace and forgiveness. At the very least there is some uncertainty about the outcome:

> [Prospero's] final decision to forgive his enemies is foreshadowed by the care he takes to save them from shipwreck, and, later, to prevent the murder of Alonso; but his decision to forgive is surely not a foregone conclusion. He will come to that resolution only when he remembers that it is precisely because of the legacy of evil, which even his art is powerless to eradicate, that man stands in need of compassion and forgiveness.[25]

The extreme view is that Prospero's intention throughout was revenge (or justice) not forgiveness and that he is converted from his purpose only at the very last. Many critics emphasise Prospero's vengefulness, particularly in the final movement of the play:

> Prospero and Ariel enter like hunters to set a pack of 'Spirits, in shape of dogs and hounds' upon [Stephano, Trinculo and Caliban], two of them bearing the names 'Fury' and 'Tyrant'. The hounds embody the wrath of Prospero, and something like vindictiveness, as he

congratulates himself on having all his 'enemies' at his mercy, and summons goblins to torture Stephano, Trinculo and Caliban, and 'grind their joints. With dry convulsions' (l. 257). Now, at the beginning of Act v, Ariel reports on the King, Alonso, and his followers, and by a nice touch prompts Prospero to mercy. . . . Prospero accepts the hint, and, while admitting to 'fury', the word echoing the name of the hound in the previous scene, he renounces his anger.[26]

As Shakespeare progressively explores other aspects of Prospero than that of the benign superhuman mage, the most significant development is from the Prospero who, in a symbolic sense, *is* God to an all-too-human Prospero who is *playing* God with people's lives. The consequences of his assumption of the right to do this are not just distasteful (as in his eavesdropping on Ferdinand and Miranda), they are potentially disastrous. In arrogating to himself the function of God, he comes very close to taking over the function of the Devil as well.

This line of thought has been elaborated by Robert Egan,[27] who argues that Prospero's intention to purge away the evil from the inhabitants of the island is flawed in its inception through his failure to see that the total eradication of evil is impossible. Prospero views humanity naïvely in terms of absolute good and absolute evil: if they are not to be the one, they must be transformed into the other. His incredulity at his brother's treachery showed his inability to accept that evil is an inevitable part of human life. The decision to use his magic art to create a totally regenerated world is a mistake with potentially tragic consequences. He conceives of himself as a god rather than a man. He mistakes his own passionate resentment of his wrongs for righteous indignation, and so the impulse to revenge threatens to become over-mastering. The masque in Act iv is an embodiment of the world he wants to create through his art: ordered but sterile, lacking in any spontaneous unruly vitality. It cannot co-exist with reality, and is broken off suddenly with the arrival of the conspirators, Caliban, Stephano and Trinculo. Prospero's reaction is one of nihilistic despair followed by rage and the intention of inflicting further torments: 'I will plague them all,/Even to roaring' (iv i 192–3). Disaster, however, is averted by Ariel, who appeals on behalf of Alonso and the others to Prospero's 'nobler reason', and so he is finally able to accept and forgive the evildoers on the basis of what he and they have in common, their flawed humanity.

A Prospero intending forgiveness and a Prospero set on revenge: these, in extreme form, are what is offered in the A and B versions of *The Tempest*. Their dual presence has not gone entirely unnoticed:

> in the attempt to make the plot more theatrical, Shakespeare has slightly confused it. If we are to judge by Prospero's arrangement of Miranda's and Ferdinand's betrothal and the conclusion of Ariel's 'harpy' speech (III iii 81–2), he intends forgiveness of his enemies from the start. But at the moment of its announcement, Prospero's forgiveness is made to look as if it were the result of a sudden change of mind (v i 21–32).[28]

In tacit recognition of this incompatibility Shakespeare retreated into the inexplicitness noted earlier, an inexplicitness which is most marked in the matter of Prospero's 'project'. For all that it is referred to several times during the action, the extraordinary fact is that we cannot say with certainty what it is. The references are cryptic in the extreme; in this central area of the play Prospero's thoughts are hidden from us. One part of the project, evident from the first act, is the bringing together and eventual betrothal of Miranda and Ferdinand. As to what is to be done with his old enemies we can only guess. Prospero refers explicitly neither to revenge nor to forgiveness; his most urgently expressed need is to have his enemies in his power, and to what this will form the prelude is left unstated. A third possibility is that Prospero himself does not know what he going to do and that he makes up his mind only at the end of the play. But the evidence fails to point unequivocally to this interpretation any more than it does to the other two. It may be consistent with any of them taken singly. That is not the same thing.

The crucial piece of evidence for these various interpretations is the exchange between Prospero and Ariel in Act v:

> ARIEL   Your charm so strongly works 'em
>   That if you now beheld them your affections
>   Would become tender.
> PROSPERO   Dost thou think so, spirit?
> ARIEL   Mine would, sir, were I human.
> PROSPERO   And mine shall.
>   Hast thou, which art but air, a touch, a feeling
>   Of their afflictions, and shall not myself,
>   One of their kind, that relish all as sharply,

Passion as they, be kindlier mov'd than thou art?
Though with their high wrongs I am struck to th' quick,
Yet with my nobler reason 'gainst my fury
Do I take part; the rarer action is
In virtue than in vengeance; they being penitent,
The sole drift of my purpose doth extend
Not a frown further. Go release them, Ariel . . . .

(v i 17–30)

This exchange at one level is perfectly simple: Prospero is announcing his intention to forgive his enemies. But that is the trouble: he announces it. The speech is oddly impersonal, and what it does not do is create the sense of a clearly defined personality responding to a particular situation. What little sense we get of an individual voice seems, if anything, to work against the grain of what is being said. 'The rarer action is / In virtue than in vengeance . . . .' A noble sentiment no doubt, but in its context it sounds uncomfortably like self-congratulation. Or is that reading too much into it? Are these wooden tones meant to preclude such close scrutiny?

The barrier between us and Prospero here is a real one. Not for the first time in the play Shakespeare has rendered him psychologically opaque, and thus where we cannot see we are obliged to infer. In this exchange between Prospero and Ariel Shakespeare has performed a minor miracle of technique, writing it in a way that is consistent with a Prospero who is dissuaded by Ariel from the path of revenge and with a Prospero who intended forgiveness all the time. Much depends on how he speaks two crucial phrases: 'Dost thou think so, spirit?' and 'And mine shall.' Assuming Prospero is intent on revenge up to that moment, 'Dost thou think so, spirit?' may be spoken either sharply or meditatively – Ariel is suggesting something that had not so far occurred to him – and Prospero's next words, 'And mine shall', coming perhaps after a short pause, are spoken resolutely as he comes to his moment of decision. But, assuming he does not need to be reminded about the plight of Alonso and the others, 'Dost thou think so, spirit?' expresses surprise, perhaps of a schoolmasterly-ironic kind,[29] that Ariel has such insight into what human beings feel. In the same way, 'And mine shall' is designed to soothe and reassure. The rest of the speech is finely balanced in its inconsistency. If we had *only* the central part with its talk of the conflict of 'reason' and 'fury', 'virtue' and 'vengeance', we should be entitled to conclude that Prospero was finally overcoming a passionate impulse to revenge himself for the 'high wrongs' he had suffered. Whereas if we had *only* the last two and a half lines ('they being penitent,/The sole drift of my purpose doth extend/Not a frown further. . . .'), their literal meaning makes it clear that forgiveness, not revenge, had been his secret 'project' throughout. But having both we must decide for ourselves where the emphasis is to fall.

There is a final point to be made about this speech. On either view proposed, the basis on which further punishments are remitted and the hand of reconciliation extended is that all the malefactors are, as Prospero says, 'penitent'. Unfortunately, they are not. What is more, Prospero at this stage has no grounds even for thinking they are penitent. All Ariel has told him is that they are 'distracted' (v i 12) – likely enough in view of everything that has happened to them since we last saw them at the end of Act III, Sebastian and Antonio wildly challenging all the legions of hell. But Prospero treats 'distracted' as if it meant 'penitent'. Why? Psychological explanations are absurd (he misheard what Ariel said?). The real explanation lies elsewhere, in the conflicts of Shakespeare's original design. The Prospero in whom he became most interested is the one we are left with at the end, the complex human being rather than the superhuman mage. Prospero has achieved something, not least perhaps in the victory over himself whereby forgiveness finally drove out the impulse to revenge. With the others he has achieved far less than he had hoped. In the 1978 Stratford production Michael Hordern spoke the line 'And they shall be themselves' (i 32) with a weight of defeated emphasis on the last word. Prospero has been preparing himself for this moment for a long time, as Ralph Berry points out: 'The recessional, the slow movement away from power begins in Act IV.'[30] Alonso has come through his trials a better man, even if the same can hardly be said for the others. Prospero recognises that no universal moral transformation has occurred, and the reconciliation with his brother, discussed in the opening chapter, is muted at best. But it is precisely that universal moral transformation that the Prospero of Shakespeare's idealising imagination was to have achieved. '. . . they being penitent' was to have been no less than literal truth. The phrase does not correspond with what the play finally shows us about the limitations of Prospero's endeavours; it is there as a belated outcropping of a simpler and vastly more optimistic conception than Shakespeare was eventually able or willing to dramatise.

VI

The identification of Prospero with Shakespeare himself has a long history. It is not difficult to see why it survived the excesses of the nineteenth-century allegorical tradition, in which Prospero's speech of farewell to his art was perhaps over-confidently seen as Shakespeare's farewell to the stage. Prospero's magic art is bound to suggest comparisons with that of the dramatist. But the comparison is closer than that. Prospero actually *is* a dramatist. He wrote the part which Ariel, transformed into a harpy, delivered to the 'three men of sin', and he was there as an audience to applaud it. He also conceived, wrote and directed the masque that dominates Act IV, a 'vanity of mine art', as he termed it (IV i 41), which he put on for the benefit of Ferdinand and Miranda.

The self-deprecatory term 'vanity' is significant. That theatrical art is no more than illusion is a possibility Shakespeare was willing to entertain throughout his career. In *The Tempest* it is given unforgettable expression in Prospero's reflections on 'the baseless fabric of this vision' that follow the interruption of the masque. But the masque will not do as a symbol of Shakespeare's own theatrical art. The fragility of Prospero's creation, its remoteness from human experience, its thin, disembodied quality – all this answers to something in *The Tempest* – specifically the tendency towards abstraction and idealisation – but not to Shakespeare's art as a whole. The order celebrated in the masque depends for its existence upon the exclusion of such as Caliban; it trembles and dissolves at his approach. It is true that there is a parallel tendency in the play itself to reject Caliban and what he symbolises. But part of his symbolic potency is that he cannot be categorised simply as the forces of brutish anarchy; the undisciplined, unchannelled energies of Caliban are, paradoxically, at a deeper, more impersonal level, the source of life itself. The masque does not sum up all of *The Tempest*, and *The Tempest* does not sum up all of Shakespeare. David Grene indicates how much is excluded even from the limited order that the masque does achieve:

Ariel, Caliban (above all Caliban), and the scenes involving the clowns on the island – which seem to have cut loose from the sketchy requirements of the plot and possess a quality all their own. The emphasis is certainly on material that defies the final transformation by the will of the manipulator. The defiance takes shape as an

exuberance of vitality, nearly monstrous, of beauty utterly beyond
rational analysis, of the warmth of laughter among ugliness and
cruelty. The beauty, the laughter, or the ugliness is always moving
out of bounds.[31]

The correspondence between Prospero and Shakespeare that suggests itself to me most forcefully is that, just as Prospero is unable finally
to establish a comprehensive harmony and eradicate all that makes for
discord in life, so too Shakespeare fails to create a satisfying aesthetic
harmony out of the world of the play. The failure by the one to create a
moral order corresponds to the inability of the other to create an artistic
order. Prospero's rage at the recalcitrance of human nature, which
remains as it is despite his efforts at reform, is analogous to, and maybe
the unconscious expression of, a similar rage by Shakespeare at what is
overwhelming in human experience, its disorganised multifariousness,
its tendency to be 'always moving out of bounds'. The promptings of his
own creativity meant that he could not avert his eyes from it; but, once
perceived, it continually resisted his efforts to shape and contain it
within an artistic framework. In *The Tempest* he had, in part, tried to
avert his eyes, experimenting fitfully with the possibility of a play based
on simplified paradigms of human nature. But the other creative
impulse behind the play ensured that the work expanded and
deepened, most of all in the presentation of its chief character. The
masque remains as an impotent symbol of what Shakespeare was
unwilling to settle for. What takes its place is vaster in scope: a larger,
more significant, more internally contradictory work, which has
nevertheless a far greater truth to experience. But there is no use
pretending it has the qualities of formal unity and perfect design.

Something of what *The Tempest* signifies is hinted at in the elliptical
comments about human life made by Stein in *Lord Jim*:

A man that is born falls into a dream like a man who falls into the sea.
If he tries to climb out into the air as inexperienced people endeavour
to do, he drowns – *nicht wahr?* . . . No! I tell you! The way is to the
destructive element submit yourself, and with the exertions of your
hands and feet in the water make the deep, deep sea keep you up.[32]

The impulse to climb out into the air corresponds to Shakespeare's
idealising impulse, the desire to rise above life as it actually is, to
abstract from it and thereby to create the 'insubstantial pageant' that

The Tempest part of the time seems to provide. To climb out into the air is to climb onto the comfort and security of Prospero's island, surrounded by the sea and safe from it. But the sea represents life, and Shakespeare's truest dramatic instinct is to do as Stein suggests – 'make the deep, deep sea keep you up'. While it may be the destructive element, it is also – vast, inexhaustible, perpetually in movement – the source and support of life itself, creative and destructive both.

5 Shakespeare: A Survey

If I start out to write a play, I start by an act of choice: I settle upon a particular emotional situation, out of which characters and a plot will emerge, and I can make a plain prose outline of the play in advance – however much that outline may be altered before the play is finished, by the way in which the characters develop. It is likely, of course, that it is in the beginning the pressure of some rude unknown psychic material that directs the poet to tell that particular story, to develop that particular situation. And on the other hand, the frame, once chosen, within which the author has elected to work, may itself evoke other psychic material; and then, lines of poetry may come into being, not from the original impulse, but from a secondary stimulus of the unconscious mind. All that matters is, that in the end the voices should be heard in harmony.[1]

Although T. S. Eliot is talking here mainly about his own creative process, there are certain similarities between this account of the gestation and composition of his work and what I take to be the shaping processes of Shakespeare's plays. Shakespeare too reveals a continuous tension between the external demands of form and the pressure from within of 'other psychic material'. While Shakespeare, like Eliot, is concerned that 'in the end the voices should be heard in harmony', unlike Eliot he does not seem to believe that this is all that matters; artistic harmony is an important but not necessarily paramount consideration. What I have tried to describe in the preceding chapters is Shakespeare's sensitivity to the implications of his dramatic material. It is of course impossible to know how much of what Shakespeare eventually wrote was planned in advance, how simple or complex was his original conception of any particular play, how various and diverse were the possible ways in which he felt the material might be developed. One needs to insist simultaneously on Shakespeare's conscious, deliberate care in the planning and execution of his plays and the possibility at least that some 'secondary impulse' in the act of writing may have deepened, challenged or started to transform what he wrote. If the plays are complex, it is because Shakespeare intended that they should be so. But the sympathy and intuitive insight, as well as profound intelligence, which he brought to his imagined characters and situations allow the possibility of fresh discoveries and new perspectives before each play is finished.

If what I have described are fundamental characteristics of Shakespeare, they should be evident throughout his work and not just in the plays discussed so far. Since it is hardly practical to analyse all the plays, I propose to look briefly, in their order of composition, at four, chosen to illustrate the main genres of comedy, history, 'problem play' and tragedy. What distinguishes a problem play from other forms of Shakespearean drama has long been a matter of debate. My purpose in discussing one from this ill-defined group is not to emphasise its distinctness but rather to show that its allegedly problematic features are present in the rest of Shakespeare's work.

The Merchant of Venice

Romantic comedy is the basic structure of *The Merchant of Venice*, in that the play begins with love and ends with the celebrations of marriage. From the point of view of the plot Shylock can be regarded as a temporary obstacle to the consummation of the one in the other. But the play is not a conventional romantic comedy, both because there is surprisingly little comedy in it, and because the marriages occur, untraditionally, half-way through, and not at the end. The fact that almost the whole of the fourth act is then given over to Shylock is a sign of his intended prominence, and the heightened drama of the trial scene itself raises the question (if it had not occurred already) of whether 'romantic comedy' is an adequate term for such a play.

No doubt *The Merchant of Venice* reinforced the expectations of many of the play's original audience by seeming to re-create in Shylock the villainous Jew of popular imagination as a foil to the virtuous Venetians. Preceding Shylock on the Elizabethan stage was the superlatively evil Barabas of Marlowe's *Jew of Malta*, and if that were not enough there was the possible influence of the notorious trial and execution two years earlier of Queen Elizabeth's physician, Roderigo

Lopez, a Portugese Jew. Shylock's acquisitiveness and crabbed harshness of manner and spirit are set against the Venetians' generosity, both
material and emotional, which finds expression in out-going cheerfulness, warm good-fellowship and hospitality. Where Shylock hoards his
gains, Antonio lays open his 'extremest means' (I i 138) to his friend
Bassanio. Portia too makes her newly married husband's concerns her
own, and offers money and the resourcefulness of a generous nature to
save her husband's friend. Bassanio is sketched in more lightly; his is a
passive role for much of the play; but he is its chief embodiment of the
spirit of romantic love, and to that end is willing to 'give and hazard all
he hath'. (II vii 16)

Yet Shylock displays – and surely was intended to display – an
impressiveness and dramatic complexity which go beyond what would
be required by such a black-and-white conception of the play and his
presumed function within it. The play was entered in the Stationers'
Register in 1598 with the alternative titles of *Merchant of Venice* and *Jew
of Venice*. It was referred to under this second name in the eighteenth
century, and the part of Shylock became the vehicle for great actors in
the nineteenth and twentieth centuries. (No actor given the choice of
Shylock and Antonio is likely to choose the latter.) Quite apart from the
passionate intensity of his presence, Shylock also serves to draw into
uncomfortably sharp focus some of the less admirable aspects of
Venetian society.

A certain shallowness in that society is apparent in the opening scene,
where the young Venetians can be not unfairly regarded as so many
amiable spendthrifts, the two things round which their lives revolve
being, on the one hand, love and friendship, and, on the other, wealth.
In this atmosphere Antonio's unaccountable melancholy appears a
solecism, a source of social embarrassment. It prompts the question,
first, if it is owing to his business worries and, secondly, if he is in love.
When these two possibilities are dismissed, no others are raised. The
connection between love and wealth is emphasised later in the scene
when Bassanio borrows money from Antonio on the grounds that only if
he has 'means' is it possible for him to try to obtain Portia's hand. This is
a purely self-imposed requirement; there is no reason why a penniless
gentleman should not present himself at Belmont as Portia's suitor. But
he wants, understandably enough, to cut a dash. He has borrowed
money before and lost it, and he tells Antonio of his present love-suit in
terms that lightly hint at his financial difficulties: 'In Belmont is a lady
richly left' (I i 161) are his first words. Nothing either here or later

suggests that Bassanio is anything as vulgar as a fortune-hunter. But financial considerations obtrude on the audience's attention in this scene, as they do throughout the play.

As the play goes on, Shakespeare starts to uncover in the Venetians the vestiges of an attitude to people and wealth not so very dissimilar from those of the man they most abhor. This is achieved in part through Shakespeare's major addition to his sources, Shylock's daughter Jessica. On the face of it she fits very well into the romance framework: the oppressed daughter escaping from domestic tyranny to the haven of a Christian marriage. We would warm to her elopement more, however, if she were less concerned to finance the start of her married life with the contents of her father's jewel-box. In a way the theft might be easier to accept if she were less casual about it – if she were to take the jewels as recompense for years of harshness and unhappiness. But there is nothing to suggest this. The theft is a matter of moral indifference to her, and her sense of delicacy and shame is confined to the temporary page-boy disguise she has to adopt. Later on we learn that she spent eighty ducats in one night at Genoa, and that she had exchanged a ring of great sentimental value to her father for a monkey. By the end of the play it is all gone, and the news of Shylock's enforced deed of gift draws from Lorenzo the relieved comment, 'you drop manna in the way / Of starved people' (v i 294–5).

With the partial exception of Antonio, the Christians, whom Jessica has elected to join, are given neither to introspection nor self-doubt. They stand well in their own esteem, conscious of their unquestionable moral superiority to Shylock. If we take them on their own terms – and to a degree the play incites us to do so – we do not question it either. But there is that in the play which *does* encourage a more sceptical view. It is partly present in the action; Jessica's making off with her father's money is capable of raising an eyebrow, even though the matter is hardly treated as a major issue. Criticism of the Venetians is also expressed much more explicitly through the mouth of Shylock himself.

Shylock is more than a figure of passionate outrage and rapacious cruelty. He can see the Venetians – and himself too – with an awkward clarity, so that through him the consciousness of the play enlarges; and once thus enlarged it becomes very difficult to restrict it again. Difficult at least to narrow it once more to what is proper to the romantic-comedy framework. The outburst of frustration and rage in which he justifies his revenge goes beyond merely giving our feelings a jolt; it begins to alter the balance of the entire play:

If you poison us, do we not die? And if you wrong us, shall we not revenge? If we are like you in the rest, we shall resemble you in that. If a Jew wrong a Christian, what is his humility? Revenge. If a Christian wrong a Jew, what should his sufferance be by Christian example? Why, revenge.   (III i 55–61)

That none of this is empty rhetoric is made clear in the trial scene, where Gratiano, the cheerful chatter-box of Act I, is transformed into a zestful Jew-baiter. A further parallel between Christian and Jew is raised in the same scene. Contemptuous of the appeals to him to show mercy, Shylock draws a mocking parallel between his right to a pound of Antonio's flesh and the rights exercised by the Venetians over their slaves:

> What judgement shall I dread, doing no wrong?
> You have among you many a purchas'd slave,
> Which, like your asses and your dogs and mules,
> You use in abject and in slavish parts,
> Because you bought them; shall I say to you
> 'Let them be free . . .'? You will answer
> 'The slaves are ours'. So do I answer you:
> The pound of flesh which I demand of him
> Is dearly bought, 'tis mine, and I will have it.
>
> (IV i 89–100)

This is plainly not a matter to be debated very much further. With a sure dramatic sense Shakespeare hurries on immediately to the arrival of Nerissa and her announcement of the supposed Balthazar. Antonio is saved, and the vile Jew discomfited. But no one answers Shylock's charge that there is no absolute moral division between him and the Venetians. For this reason the Duke's 'That thou shalt see the difference of our spirit' (IV i 363), as he pardons Shylock, rings faintly hollow; it both does and does not establish such a difference. The reverberations of this scene continue to trouble us after Shylock's departure – a reaction which is increased rather than diminished by the Venetians' consciousness of their own rectitude.

Despite the beautiful other-worldly lyricism of the scene between Lorenzo and Jessica that opens Act V, the remainder of the play is often felt as something of an anti-climax. The practical joke with the rings Shakespeare inherited from his main source along with the bond plot, its superficial merriment providing, in the original story, a comic conclusion to the whole. In some measure it serves that function in Shakespeare's play as well. But in dramatising what is a rather obvious and external comic plot Shakespeare seems to have tapped deeper levels, so that it becomes the vehicle for something with more human interest: the conflict of male friendship and married love; and it is here that the interest of the rest of the play lies.

Antonio, in giving his money and risking his life for the sake of his friend, can be seen as a pattern of selfless generosity – a generosity which can claim a rare disinterestedness if we note the depth of feeling for Bassanio implied in Solanio's casual judgement 'I think he only loves the world for him' (II viii 50). The importance Antonio attaches to their friendship probably lies behind the mysterious melancholy he admits to at the beginning of the play. Its origins are suggested by his first words to Bassanio when they are alone:

> Well; tell me now what lady is the same
> To whom you swore a secret pilgrimage,
> That you to-day promis'd to tell me of? (I i 119–21)

Antonio is preparing to relinquish the major share in Bassanio's affections to Portia; and he does so freely and without fuss. But a different, less detached, note is sounded in the letter which Antonio writes to Bassanio from prison:

> Sweet Bassanio, my ships have all miscarried, my creditors grow cruel, my estate is very low, my bond to the Jew is forfeit; and since, in paying it, it is impossible I should live, all debts are clear'd between you and I, if I might but see you at my death. Notwithstanding, use your pleasure; if your love do not persuade you to come, let not my letter. (III ii 317–22)

The appeal that is made here is all the more poignant for the evident attempt at its suppression. Even so, the last two lines barely avoid the effect of emotional blackmail.

Bassanio, who much of the play has simply been the happy beneficiary of Antonio's efforts on his behalf, reveals in the trial scene the extent of what Antonio means to him. At the climactic moment when it seems that Antonio must die, he and Gratiano announce that they would sacrifice both themselves and their newly married wives so that Antonio might live. Its immediate effect is perhaps less dramatic than comic. Portia's presence reassures us that Antonio's rescue cannot now be long delayed, and the irony of the offer is promptly underscored by the pert comments of Portia and Nerissa: 'your wife would give you little thanks for that,/If she were by to hear you make the offer'(IV i 283–4). But the moment can hardly be other than disconcerting for them, and in this context the episode of the rings ceases to be a mere gratuitous piece of comic deception. It is the means by which Portia and Nerissa, through making their husbands feel guilty and uncomfortable, assert their claims to their husbands' love over that of Antonio. But expressing it thus is misleading, in that it gives an over-explicit emphasis to what Shakespeare largely leaves as a matter of hints and suggestions. Nerissa enters into the spirit of the thing more as a game than anything else. Only in Portia's case do we have the occasional sense that something more serious is at stake.

In the portrayal of Portia there is the suggestion of a fairy-tale *princesse lointaine*, bound by the will of her dead father, and eventually claimed by her true prince, to whom she offers herself in love and submission:

> her gentle spirit
> Commits itself to yours to be directed,
> As from her lord, her governor, her king.   (III ii 164–6)

But much closer to the surface is a woman of considerable character, wit, authority and intelligence, bored at the beginning of the play by inactivity, chafing under the conditions of her father's will, and quite capable of putting a glass of wine by the wrong casket to mislead a sottish suitor. Later on she is capable also of playing what, from one point of view, is a game of cat-and-mouse with Shylock in the trial scene. There is more than one way of taking her much-anthologised 'quality of mercy' speech (IV i 179–200). Superficially it helps to define the essential difference between the spirit of Christian mercy appealed to by the Venetians and the inhuman vengefulness of Shylock. At the same time its set-piece quality is faintly suspicious; much of it sounds like an aria to the abstract notion of mercy rather than an appeal made in hope of its practical effect on Shylock; and it ends with a wholly incorrect piece of legal advice – her confirmation of 'the justice of thy plea,/Which if thou follow, this strict court of Venice/Must needs give sentence 'gainst the merchant there'. At the time she says it we accept the statement as fact. In retrospect we have to decide whether Portia's

hastily mugged-up knowledge of the law had temporarily deserted her
or whether it was a deliberate lie designed to give Shylock a false sense of
security. What we decide here has a bearing on a larger question: was
Portia's eventual thwarting of Shylock a sudden happy improvisation
or the conclusion of a strategy carefully prepared in advance? The
romantic view of Portia suggests the former; the realistic view – and the
general weight of evidence – suggests the latter.

On either view the trial scene reveals her as sharp-witted and
combative. Her husband's hyperbolical declaration of what he would
do to save Antonio leaves her in no doubt. She has a rival.

Although the triangular relationship of Antonio, Bassanio and Portia
may strike us as idyllic and uncomplicated, what also interests
Shakespeare are tensions below the idyllic surface, stemming from
emotional insecurity and loss. For Antonio the loss of Bassanio is real
and irreversible. For Portia it is only a potential threat. Even without
what she had heard in the trial scene, Bassanio's parting with his ring
could hardly have seemed to her a trivial matter. What she had given
him in Belmont was not merely her love but – something she herself
referred to at the time – all her possessions. In return she had received
the promise of his love, symbolised by the ring. An unequal exchange
perhaps, and one where the ring was bound to assume a large and even
disproportionate emotional significance. But in the final scene
Shakespeare is careful not to allow these under-currents to flow too close
to the surface; the prevailing tone is cheerful and comic rather than
tense and acrimonious. The briskness of the comedy is nevertheless
given a certain edge by the fact that, despite the courteous welcome
extended to Antonio, Portia's attitude is less than effusive. She says little
to him throughout, and her manner may be a trifle brusque when she
replies to his rather ineffectual 'I am th' unhappy subject of these
quarrels' with a short 'Sir, grieve not you; you are welcome notwith-
standing' (IV i 198–200). Had she known it was he who had actually
persuaded Bassanio to part with the ring, the welcome might have been
a good deal more chilly. As it is, she seizes on his piously expressed hope
that Bassanio will never again break faith with her, and adds with some
satisfaction, handing him the original ring,

> Then you shall be his surety. Give him this,
> And bid him keep it better than the other.   (v i 254–5)

At the end of the play Antonio learns that his ships, thought lost, are safely returned. His relief at the news is reinforced a few lines later by Lorenzo's joyfulness when he hears that he is to inherit Shylock's property. In such an uncynical but not unwordly play virtue does not have to be its own reward, and on this note of financial as well as emotional satisfaction the romantic comedy comes to an appropriate close.

Henry V

After the insistence by earlier criticism that Shakespeare's histories should be seen in relation to each other, recent studies have paid more attention to the individuality of the separate plays, particularly those of the second tetralogy. The differences in style and structure of *Richard II*, the *Henry IV* plays and *Henry V* are at least as significant as any common dramatic purpose they may be assumed to possess. The treatment of *Henry V* was largely dictated by the stock sixteenth-century response to its hero, derived from both the Chronicle histories and existing dramatic versions of his reign. It is possible also that Shakespeare may have felt constrained by the logic of his portrayal of Henry V at the end of *Henry IV, Part 2*: the king who is celebrated there requires a blinkered response and short memory if we are to endorse his final characterisation of Falstaff as 'The tutor and the feeder of my riots' (v v 63).

Whatever the strength of these pressures, Shakespeare turned them to good account by experimenting with a history play markedly different from its predecessors. In writing about the miraculous victory at Agincourt, a battle where, one of his sources alleged, only twenty-five English were slain as against ten thousand French, he embarked on a work of national myth-making, epic in scope; and an inevitable part of this conception was that the play should be a panegyric to a Henry who was brave, warlike, pious and just. At the same time, given the play as we have it, this was plainly not all Shakespeare was setting out to do. He was drawn to exploring a more sceptical, less exclusively laudatory view of the enterprise and its central character. The degree to which such additional perspectives were planned in advance is a matter of speculation, though their presence is sufficiently ubiquitous to suggest considerable prior thought. A more critically relevant question is how far these additional viewpoints are integrated into a work operating much of the time at a different level. For *Henry V*, it seems to me, is a play of unabsorbed ambiguities.

The epic dimension to the play, involving an uncomplicated appeal to national sentiment, is readily apparent. The legitimacy of Henry's claim to the French throne is not questioned by anyone in the play – least of all by Henry himself, even when, before Agincourt, he expresses contrition for 'the fault / My father made in compassing the crown' (IV i 289–90). Equally there is not the slightest hint that his presence in France is in response to his father's advice in *Henry IV, Part 2* 'to busy giddy minds / With foreign quarrels' (IV v 214–15). The play's progress in an unbroken line to the anticipated triumph at Agincourt combines the premonitory tremors of possible disaster with the satisfaction of a glorious victory. And, just as in the hour of danger the little band of English soldiers closes ranks behind the King, so too does the audience: now is not the time to start entertaining queasy philosophical doubts about the legitimacy of the whole campaign and the morality of its instigator. *Henry V*'s main appeal is to the eye and ear, not the intellect. The presence of the Chorus at the beginning of each act has the effect of transforming the play into a series of tableaux: Henry defying the Dauphin in Act I; the unmasking of the conspirators in Act II; the siege of Harfleur in Act III; the 'little touch of Harry in the night' and the Crispin's Day speech in Act IV; the wooing of Katherine in Act V. The Chorus's introduction beating the patriotic drum sets the prevailing tone; and significantly, in his introduction to Act I, he refers to Agincourt in terms which assume that the audience already knows the basic story. None of the other history plays gives away so much in advance – or, rather, takes so much for granted. It lends a carnival air to the occasion, as the audience prepares to be excited and entertained by a well-known and well-loved tale.

The humour of the play reinforces the patriotic tone. All nationalities other than the English are patronised; the Welsh, Scots and Irish are treated with humorous indulgence, the French with humorous contempt. There is an inevitable reliance on national stereotypes. We are invited to have an appreciatively good-natured chuckle at the fiery leek-eating Welshman, Fluellen, at the dour Scot, Jamy, and the quarrelsome Irishman, Macmorris. The coming together of England's traditional enemies to make common cause against France testifies further to Henry's capacity to unify his kingdom. Even their accents sound odd and faintly amusing to English ears. Equally amusing is the attempt of foreigners to speak our language, which explains the inclusion of Katherine's English lesson. Later on the jabbering, gesticulating, cowardly M. Le Fer is captured by, of all people, Pistol,

the most cowardly soldier in Henry's army. Some of the play's humour
is directed back at the English, as in the Constable's jibes about
England's climate, 'foggy, raw, and dull' (III v 16), its dirty farms and
barley broth. But this is just inverted self-compliment. The audience
can afford to smile at the insults – our peasant origins attest to our
superior virility, as the Dauphin himself admits. We can even later on
relax and laugh at Henry's half-baked attempt to speak French in his
wooing of Katherine: after all, we *won*. Henry's wooing also deploys the
English stereotype of the blunt, honest, straightforward soul of strong
feelings and few words – whether or to what extent Henry is deliberately
acting a role here it is impossible to tell. Again the performance invites a
complacent warm-hearted chuckle, and again there is something
offensive about self-directed humour which is so entirely unbarbed and
self-approving.

Where the humour is not of this kind, it is mostly practical jokes and
knock-about, as in Henry's jest concerning the gage which involved
Fluellen and Williams, or the forcing of Pistol by Fluellen to swallow the
detested leek. The humour of *Henry V* is of a piece with the play's overt
aim of extolling the victor of Agincourt. It is broad in effect but not
broad in scope. Falstaff is killed off, and with his death the free-ranging
comic spirit which played to such effect over the *Henry IV* plays dies too.
Comedy now enlists as a soldier in Henry's army. It supports and
sustains; it does not question. It is no longer associated with the active
play of a sceptical intelligence which Falstaff's presence, far more than
anything he actually said, stimulated in *Henry IV*. With Falstaff around
it was impossible to take any politician entirely seriously or exclusively
on his own terms. With his death there is no likelihood that comedy will
blow even the quietest of raspberries amid the general chorus of
adulation.

Nevertheless, the play as finally written is an unintegrated work,
something more and less than the work of patriotic glorification so far
described. Most of the critical debate about this play, and the
remarkably diverse responses to it, are a tacit recognition of this central
fact. Many critics have been uncomfortable about the play's surface
impressions on a variety of moral or artistic grounds. Surely the play is
not meant to reveal Shakespeare's awe-struck admiration of a warrior-
king. Surely too his heart is not in it when he arranges for the
conspirators against Henry to be led off, not in sullen defiance as in
earlier plays, but – incredibly – offering pious thanks for their apprehension. There is no point looking for suggestions of irony

here. Part of the play had been conceived in a spirit of glorifying Henry, and the dramatic effect of such occasions is not such as to invite pause and examination. *Henry V* did not set out to offer the realistic exploration of men and motives that took place in *Henry IV*. Its surface is hard and unyielding; the play (to change the metaphor) does not put down deep roots. Quite apart from a distaste for jingoism, the sense of constriction is, I imagine, one reason why many people are not at home with the play and do not care for it very much. The fact is, however, that ironies, qualifications and the suggestion of a larger vision do exist in *Henry V*, but they are not – and in the nature of the undertaking perhaps could not have been – integrated into a comprehensive, warts-and-all portrayal of its hero.

There are two main areas which Shakespeare seems to have felt impelled to develop despite what it might do to the play's final effect. One was the human cost of war; the other, obviously related, was the extent of the King's responsibility for it. The former had its origins in the plays that preceded *Henry V*. Shakespeare is here merely developing what he had already started. In *Henry IV, Part 1* the anonymous 'food for powder' troop across the stage on their way to 'fill a pit as well as better' (IV ii 63–4). In the recruiting scenes in Gloucestershire in *Part 2*, Shakespeare gives them names, faces, personalities, families. In *Henry V* he goes one stage further and shows them bracing themselves for the coming battle, for killing or being killed.

The common soldiers in this play form two distinct groups. One is Falstaff's tatterdemalion crew of hangers-on, Bardolph, Nym and Pistol. Shakespeare appears not entirely comfortable with this visible reminder of Henry's salad days, and they are picked off one by one during the course of the play. Not, however, before they establish themselves as representative of an attitude to war a good deal less high-principled than Henry's. Immediately after his Harfleur speech and only four lines after his exultant cry of 'I see you stand like greyhounds in the slips' (III i 31), we see Nym, Bardolph and Pistol advancing most reluctantly to the breach, and we hear the Boy express himself in tones equally as heartfelt as Henry's: 'Would I were in an alehouse in London! I would give all my fame for a pot of ale and safety' (III ii 11–12). Earlier in the play the motives of Pistol and the others for joining the expedition to France form an ironic counterpoint to Henry's reasons of state: 'Let us to France, like horse-leeches, my boys, / To suck, to suck, the very blood to suck' (II iii 55–6). The only French they seem to know (the Boy apart) is 'Couple a gorge!' (II i 69), and the motif of throat-cutting runs through the play, achieving its most memorable expression in Gower's boast, at some point in the battle, that 'the King most worthily hath caus'd every soldier to cut his prisoner's throat'; this grotesque form of praise is only made worse by his insistence, 'O, 'tis a gallant King!' (IV vii 8–10) One would like to think that some irony was intended here, but it seems doubtful.

The other group of English soldiers, Bates, Court and Williams, are treated by Shakespeare with far more respect than the cowardly, rascally Pistol and his friends. Apart from being honest, brave and loyal, they are also more intelligent, and in the night before Agincourt they unknowingly ask Henry some awkward questions about the King's responsibility.

The question which the play circles back to in the darkness before the battle is the one that Henry himself proposes at the very beginning: 'May I with right and conscience make this claim?' (I ii 96). In the absence of such a right the assault on France becomes a mere war of conquest. Superficially the play does indeed show the claim to be well founded. The King, whose piety has been emphasised in the opening scene, puts himself in the hands of the Archbishop of Canterbury, who, in the much-skipped Salic Law speech, proves that his claim is incontestable. Our only hesitations are likely to be caused by a memory of the ecclesiastical manoeuvring in the preceding scene, in which Canterbury and Ely propose to divert Henry from plundering their lands by giving religious approval to his intended invasion of France – an invasion on which, to judge from the Dauphin's sarcastic gift of tennis-balls, he seems already more than half-way embarked. It has been alleged in Henry's defence that he was unaware of the Archbishop's slightly suspect tactics. It is just as likely that he did not very much care. To say this is not to imply that the tone of the scene is overtly cynical, for it is not. But Henry's character retains one trait already in evidence in *Henry IV*: a reluctance to accept responsibility for actions which he has deliberately chosen to perform, and a corresponding desire to place responsibility for them on someone else. His association with Falstaff was the obvious case in point, for in the rejection speech he had presented himself to the world as an innocent led astray ('The *tutor* and the feeder of my riots . . . the rest of my *misleaders*' – v v 63–5). In his first scene in *Henry V* he takes a curiously passive role. He tells the Archbishop, 'Therefore take heed how you *impawn* our person' (I ii 21), and, when he asks the crucial question, 'May I with right and conscience make this claim?' the reply he receives is couched in exactly the terms he wants: 'The sin upon my head, dread sovereign!' (ll. 96–7). Later in the same scene the gift of French tennis-balls provides Henry with a further absolution. Not his but the Dauphin's soul 'Shall stand sore charged for the wasteful vengeance' (l. 283) that will ensue. 'And some are yet ungotten and unborn / That shall have cause to curse the Dauphin's scorn' (ll. 287–8). Even in dispensing justice Henry combines forthrightness with this same self-protective reticence. The exchange with Cambridge, Scroop and Grey over his proposed release of a man who had drunkenly insulted him seems to have the aim of ensuring they will invoke on themselves the full rigour of the law for their treason. 'The mercy that was quick in us but late / By your own counsel is suppress'd and kill'd' (ii ii 79–80). In the very moment of pronouncing sentence Henry is concerned to let as little responsibility as possible rest on him personally: 'Touching our person seek we no revenge' (l. 174).

This aspect of Henry's personality is never brought sharply into focus. Not surprisingly, since the play is more concerned with creating a myth than with exploring individual psychology. The one moment in the play when it seems Henry will be made to face squarely the extent of his responsibilities is the night before Agincourt. As it turns out, the issue is fudged. The debate begins promisingly enough when Henry's bland assurance about 'his cause being just and his quarrel honourable' is met with Williams's curt, 'That's more than we know' (iv i 126–8). Bates follows this with, 'If his cause be wrong, our obedience to the King wipes the crime of it out of us' (ll. 131–2), and Williams continues,

But if the cause be not good, the King himself hath a heavy reckoning to make when all those legs and arms and heads, chopp'd off in a battle, shall join together at the latter day and cry all 'We died at such a place' – some swearing, some crying for a surgeon, some upon their wives left poor behind them, some upon the debts they owe, some upon their children rawly left. I am afeard there are few die well that die in a battle; for how can they charitably dispose of anything when blood is their argument? Now, if these men do not die well, it will be a black matter for the King that led them to it; who to disobey were against all proportion of subjection.   (ll. 133–45)

This phantasmagoric evocation, both pitiful and ghastly, of the carnage caused by war merely repeats more vividly what Henry himself described earlier when he had thrust all responsibility for such carnage onto the Dauphin. Whatever the strength of his claim to the French throne, Henry's soldiers know only that they are in France in obedience to their King, and their view of the coming battle is more sharply focused on its physical horrors. That they are there at all and that on the morrow many of them will die are the result of Henry's freely taken decision. Shakespeare here seems to be juxtaposing the notion of a just war with its inevitable cost in human terms and, by implication, asking whether the one can justify the other.

The question receives no clear answer. The King's reply is long, detailed, logical and abstruse. What he does – admittedly with the help of a shift of ground in Williams's speech – is move the debate from the broadly human one of responsibility for the horrors of war to the more narrowly theological one of responsibility for the souls of those who die in battle. The confidence with which Henry marshalls his arguments, the absence of any challenge to them, the fact that Williams is either bemused or genuinely convinced, all do their work. We are left with the general, if spurious, impression that the plain man's objections to war have been raised and adequately answered, so that we can now get back and enjoy the heroics with a clear conscience.

After this uncertain attempt to encompass the dark side of war, the play becomes progressively more external again. Henry's soliloquy, 'Upon the King!' (ll. 226–80), expressing a weariness of spirit at the burdens of kingship, seems to invite a sympathetic response. At the end of the scene he prays for the withholding of vengeance over his father's part in the usurpation and murder of Richard II; and it is characteristic of Shakespeare's presentation of Henry that one hardly registers the fact that he is asking not to be held responsible for a death in which he had no part, while saying nothing about his responsibility for the vastly greater number of deaths in the coming battle. His Crispin's Day speech (IV iii 18–67) expresses an ideal of comradeship in battle which is genuinely stirring; and, indeed, from its beginnings in the King's preoccupation with honour ('if it be a sin to covet honour, / I am the most offending soul alive') it develops a rare depth and generosity of imagination, setting the terrors of the coming battle in the larger context of old men's memories and an England finally at peace. In this speech the play's central vision – an exalted patriotism – achieves its most moving and deeply felt expression. Nothing else in the play quite matches it; and the difference is perceivable later on in the externality of treatment whereby the reported deaths of York and Suffolk are presented as an implausibly rapturous apotheosis.

After the battle Burgundy, in bringing together the kings of England
and France for the first time, has a delicate situation to handle. It would
be less than tactful to accuse the conqueror to his face of the havoc he
has caused. So his account of the ravages suffered by France manages to
be both specific and yet impersonal, as if a country desolated by war had
experienced a natural calamity, not the consequences of human choice
and will. From this point Henry moves briskly into a wooing of
Katherine, the comic tone of which is likely to seem, in the context of
Burgundy's speech, irredeemably shallow. There is, finally, not a hint of
ironic awareness – the gift of historical hindsight – in the short-lived
alliance formed at the end of the play between the 'brothers' of England
and France. Even the Chorus, despite a nod to the future in his reference
to Henry VI 'in infant bands crown'd king', manages to keep a straight
face.

Measure for Measure

The development of the plot of *Measure for Measure* leaves us in little
doubt about its tragi-comic structure. After the anxieties of incipient
tragedy we experience the joy, not to say relief, of a comic conclusion.
Evil intentions come to nothing; nobody is harmed; and the would-be
sinner (Angelo), now penitent, is forgiven. The agent of this felicitous
transformation is the Duke, who, as the central character of the play,
has the greatest influence on other people's lives, an influence clearly
directed to the ultimate good of all. The implausibility of the plot and
the inherent strangeness of the Duke's disguised role suggest that the
play, if not an allegory, is a fable of some kind. A religious fable is hinted
at by the play's title – the only one taken by Shakespeare directly from
the Bible – by the many Biblical references in the play itself, and by the
fact that of its chief characters one is a novice and the other spends most
of his time disguised as a friar. It is not necessary to travel the full length
of the allegorical road and see the Duke as the representation of God. But
he is clearly separate from the other characters. His idiom at times sets
him apart (as in the powerful octosyllabics of 'He who the sword
of heaven will bear' – III ii 243–64); he is concerned to reform and
redeem the flawed humanity within his dukedom; his return inspires
a quasi-religious awe and wonder; and his judgements at the end
uphold a balance of justice and mercy, qualities which in the earlier
part of the play had existed only in the over-indulgent mercy of

Escalus and the harsh punitive legalism of Angelo.

The problems with which the Duke has to deal stem from the fact that Vienna is a city of extremes. In sexual matters it is divided between the licentiousness of Pompey, Mistress Overdone and Lucio and the asceticism of Angelo and Isabella. On the one hand the corruption of the sexual impulse through its manifestation as simple lust; on the other its more subtle corruption through the artificial reining in of natural desire. Attitudes to sexuality are a measure of attitudes to law and the maintenance of good order in society. For Pompey the law is to be flouted and evaded. For Angelo, at the other extreme, the rule of law is to be upheld in its most rigorous and legalistic form. From these extreme positions the Duke calls the various parties to a humanely ordered middle ground, an area large enough to accommodate a Claudio as representative of *l'homme moyen sensuel* without celebrating him as any kind of ideal; for Claudio, like virtually all the characters in the play, is the object of the Duke's reforming and educative spirit. The unregenerate and ultimately incorrigible members of his community, Pompey and Mistress Overdone, he leaves to be dealt with by Angelo; by the end of the play they are in jail, and the Duke is evidently disposed to leave them there. His direct influence is on those more responsive to his efforts at their improvement: Angelo, Isabella, Claudio and Juliet.

Angelo and Isabella have obvious similarities. They are by temperament authoritarian. When we see each of them for the first time, their first words show how much they are inured to habits of unquestioning obedience to authority. Angelo: 'Always obedient to your Grace's will,/ I come to know your pleasure' (1 i 26–7). And Isabella:

> And have you nuns no farther privileges?
> . . . I speak not as desiring more,
> But rather wishing a more strict restraint
> Upon the sisterhood, the votarists of Saint Clare.

> (1 iv 1–5)

In Angelo, no less than Isabella, we are conscious of the self-imposition of a 'strict restraint'; he is, according to the Duke, 'A man of stricture and firm abstinence' (1 iii 12). Denying any positive role to natural instinct in the governing of their lives, Angelo and Isabella appeal instead to abstract principle. In Isabella's case the principle is that of her chastity, the preservation of which takes precedence over all other human values, including her brother's life. In Angelo's it is, in a complementary way, the rigorous, uncompromising enforcement of the law against unchastity. Their common attitude to sex is illustrated in their belief – unchanged, so far as one can tell, even at the end of the play – that the law which condemned Claudio to death was just. Their high-principled recoil from sensuality is accompanied by an ignorance about their own sexual nature, and the first half of the play shows the consequences of this combination of self-ignorance and abstract moral fervour. The enforcement of the law against fornication leads first to Claudio's imminent execution and then to Angelo's meeting with Isabella to plead for her brother's life, a meeting which releases in him sexual desires of over-mastering intensity. Isabella in her turn, caught between Angelo's importunings and Claudio's pleading for his life, responds to these dual pressures with horror, rage and hysterical denunciation.

This is the crisis in the lives of four people which the Duke now has to solve. His aim is not just physical but spiritual redemption. Claudio is saved, but not before the Duke's speech 'Be absolute for death' (III i 5–41) brings him to a state of at least temporary equanimity. The Duke satisfies himself that Juliet too is penitent for what she has done. Angelo, unknown to himself, is saved from the consequences of his actions, and the eventual public exposure of his evil intentions leaves him wretched and remorseful. Isabella for her part has to learn the Christian virtues of compassion and forgiveness; when Angelo has been humbled and Mariana's happiness depends on her decision, she finds herself able to plead for the life of the man who had tried to violate her.

The play does not end here. It ends, in the tradition of Shakespeare's romantic comedies, with multiple marriages. Claudio is restored to Juliet; Angelo, rather less happily, to Mariana; Lucio, less still to Kate Keepdown. And the Duke offers his hand to – and in stage tradition is accepted by – Isabella. The effect of these marriages is certainly curious, since the romantic-comedy structure is not the most obvious or appropriate way of concluding the play's treatment of sin, punishment, justice and mercy. Only that of Claudio and Juliet is likely to be received by the audience in a spirit of warm, uncomplicated relief and rejoicing; they are the only couple who actually want to be married to each other; but of the four marriages it is the one to which Shakespeare gives least dramatic attention. Elsewhere marriage seems to be used by the Duke as an instrument of state whereby the virtuous and the wicked receive their due rewards, punishments and incitements to reform. Within this dispensation love itself becomes a matter of ducal fiat; 'Joy to you, Mariana! Love her, Angelo' commands the Duke in his final speech(v i 524). Undoubtedly the most startling example of the Duke's match-making is the union he proposes between himself and Isabella. There is little in the previous part of the play to prepare us for it. One may argue the symbolic appropriateness of marriage as the final step in freeing Isabella from her self-repressive concern about her chastity earlier on, but that seems a particularly tendentious piece of special pleading.

Since the ending of *Measure for Measure* strikes some faintly jarring notes in the context of what has been said so far, it is as well to be clear how much this discussion has rested on an elevated and uncritical view of the Duke. The argument up to this point assumes that he is the controlling figure in the play – controlling, that is, not only the various characters' lives but also our response to them, to everything that happens – and to himself. We are asked to see the world through his eyes; what he admires we admire; what he detests we detest. He is the structural, emotional and intellectual centre of the play. Such a view of the Duke is the result of a selective extrapolation from the play; it depends in particular upon reading back into the first part of the play what we have learned about him from the second. In fact Shakespeare's intentions with regard to the Duke are complex and elusive, and they are not such as to require us from the very beginning to identify with him.

One reason why we are initially unlikely to accept the Duke's point of view as our own is that *Measure for Measure* is a play in which it is difficult to get our bearings. Its plot rests on a highly contrived situation: after the Duke's departure his Deputy enforces an archaic law whereby, if a betrothed couple sleep together, the man risks a death sentence. Any audience, even Shakespeare's, must assume that the dramatist – surely – does not intend such a Draconian law to be applauded. Where in the play can the audience look for confirmation that this is so? Not, at all events, to the Duke. Before he departs he is talking about his unenforced laws as 'The needful bits and curbs to headstrong steeds' (i iii 20), and his later comment on lechery is that 'It is too general a vice, and severity must cure it' (iii ii 93). Is he referring merely to such people as Pompey? Or does he in fact agree with Angelo that Claudio deserves to die? His eventual efforts to save Claudio make it clear, although the evidence is too inconclusive for us to decide whether he has undergone a change of heart in the interim. At the beginning of the play we are simply floundering. Inevitably we look elsewhere. The characters who voice reactions we can identify with are Escalus ('Let us be keen, and rather cut a little / Than fall and bruise to death' – II i 5–6), the Provost ('Alas, / He hath but as offended in a dream! / All sects, all ages, smack of this vice; and he / To die for 't' – II ii 3–6), and conceivably the disreputable Lucio ('if myself might be his judge, / He should receive his punishment in thanks: / He hath got his friend with child' – I iv 27–9).

However much the Duke may be the centre of the play taken as a whole, neither his presence nor his later importance has been firmly established in the audience's eyes before Shakespeare turns with a zest and quickened imagination to the characters who dominate the first part of *Measure for Measure*. By common consent the scenes in the first three acts involving Angelo, Isabella and Claudio are the finest in the play. Because they are so compelling we are bound to have mixed feelings after the Duke steps forward at the end of Isabella's hysterical vituperation with a smooth, 'Vouchsafe a word, young sister, but one word' (III i 153). On the one hand we are meant to feel relief – and to some extent we must feel it – at the proposed solution to this complex dilemma. On the other, it is hard not to suppress a sense of disappointment that everything is being thus cut short. It is not as if we had been led to expect the Duke's intervention. There was nothing in the story (or in common sense) to suggest that he somehow knew and had predicted the precise course of events that would follow his temporary abdication, and that he was biding his time with Mariana up his sleeve, as it were, ready to intervene at the appropriate moment. Thus a situation which has a discernible human logic of its own is resolved not by the Duke's intervention but by Shakespeare's. And the means of Isabella's deliverance – the bed-trick – carries with it echoes of its origins in folk-tale and the simpler dramaturgy of Shakespeare's contemporaries. Plot material of this kind is too raw and crude for his purpose, and cannot easily be adapted to form part of the subtle, intellectual and passionate drama that *Measure for Measure* has become.

The Duke is a character whom the thrust of the play and the verdict of virtually all the characters in it call on us to admire but who nevertheless either exists only in sketchy outline or, where he ceases to be sketchy, is endowed with humanising detail that is neither attractive nor admirable. In particular Shakespeare has given the Duke some of the less attractive qualities of the very man he is subjecting to a course of moral improvement. Like Angelo the Duke is ignorant about his sexual nature and takes pride in his supposed indifference to women. When he sets out from Vienna, he emphasises to Friar Thomas that it is not for a romantic adventure:

> No, holy father; throw away that thought;
> Believe not that the dribbling dart of love
> Can pierce a complete bosom.   (i iii 1–3)

The conclusion of the play reveals the hollowness of this boast. The Duke's complacency here is the same as that recalled by Angelo after his first meeting with Isabella: 'Ever till now,/When men were fond, I smil'd and wond'red how' (ii ii 186–7). Both characters are a reworking by Shakespeare of that familiar comic type, the mocker at love who himself falls in love, and the similarity between them is emphasised by the fact that both are drawn to the same woman. A further shared characteristic is an aloofness from and (though the evidence in the Duke's case does not all point to this conclusion) an implied disdain for the common people. Most evident in Angelo, it is also there in the Duke's choice of words when he describes himself as one who has always 'held in idle price to haunt assemblies/Where youth, and cost, a witless bravery keeps' (i iii 9–10). The dismissive contempt for the pleasures of ordinary people masks a paradoxical desire to stand well in their eyes. Angelo reveals it in an early soliloquy when he refers to 'my gravity,/ Wherein – let no man hear me – I take pride' (ii iv 9–10). This kind of vanity, however, is much more evident in the Duke. He is excessively conscious of his public reputation, anxious about what people think of him, and concerned that his good name should not be slandered. We can hardly forget that his main stated reason for leaving Angelo to remedy his years of neglect is the self-protective desire that the people should not think badly of him.

A less than flawless Duke is likely to prove less than infallible as a guide to the world of the play. We may start to notice discrepancies between what he tells us and what the play itself reveals.

A major example of what I mean is the Duke's fierce condemnation of sexual vice. His characterisation of the low-life element has been taken up and endorsed by many critics:

> My business in this state
> Made me a looker-on here in Vienna,
> Where I have seen corruption boil and bubble
> Till it o'errun the stew . . . .   (v i 314–17)

But how well does this kind of language sum up Shakespeare's portrayal of the low-life characters? In *Henry IV, Part 2* he had shown the Eastcheap taverns and brothels as squalid and degrading, and in *Pericles* the brothel scenes are frightening and horrifying. But here the treatment is almost wholly comic. The scenes involving Mistress Overdone's friends and acquaintances are positively jolly; they are, if anything, genial to a fault. In the Escalus trial scene Pompey is the comedian and Elbow, a re-creation of the comic constable, Dogberry, in *Much Ado*, is his stooge. The prison scenes in the second half of the play, where we might expect a darkening of tone, treat incarceration and the gallows in a similarly comic spirit: Abhorson the executioner and Pompey as his apprentice perform a double act through Act IV. Even when Barnadine appears, we still remain cosily insulated from the realities of prison life. Condemned murderer though he is, he is yet another comic figure, taking prison on his own terms; his refusal of Pompey's invitation to come and be executed is too whimsical to count even as black comedy. There is insufficient imaginative realism to turn such an entertaining hairy monster into a symbol – whether of the brutalising effect of the Duke's failure to enforce his laws or of the unregenerate depravity in Vienna's vice-ridden society. For all the tendency of some producers to fill the prison scenes with grubby extras miming degeneracy for all they are worth, the tone of the scenes as written is really quite chirpy. In consequence the effect of the Duke's presence in these scenes is far from simple. To the extent that we are enjoying the party the Duke's tight-lipped severity may seem out of place – even faintly ridiculous.

This brings us finally to Lucio, who is a focus for the two conceptions of the Duke coexisting uneasily in the play. Those who think well of the Duke have little to say about Lucio except what is disapproving; he is a debauched frequenter of Mistress Overdone's brothels and a malicious slanderer whom the Duke quite properly puts in his place. But this ignores the extent to which the scenes where Lucio slanders the Duke are richly comic – both with and at the expense of both characters involved. We do not merely laugh at Lucio for his unconscious folly; many of his slanders about the Duke's sexually misspent past are wittily inventive, regardless of whether there is any truth to them.[2] Furthermore his jibe about 'the old fantastical Duke of dark corners' (IV iii 153–4) is an apt description of the Duke's methods if not his aims, and it is a relief for us to have our common-sense observations confirmed. What is more important, Lucio, disreputable as he no doubt is, demonstrates a spontaneous practical humanity in doing what he can to save Claudio, which shows well against the element of the calculating and manipulative in the Duke's schemes. The contrast between them is most sharply felt when Isabella receives the news (falsely manufactured by the Duke) that her brother has been executed after all. The Duke offers nothing by way of comfort, and the terms in which he urges her to compose herself are astonishingly insensitive: 'Command these fretting waters from your eyes/With a light heart' (ll. 143–4). By contrast Lucio's response has a more immediate kindness and sympathy and a greater tact: 'O pretty Isabella, I am pale at my heart to see thine eyes so red. Thou must be patient' (ll. 148–9).[3]

The Duke's tone of voice here, his attitude to Isabella, indeed his concealed purposes as a whole, are often defended according to religious or symbolic–moralistic readings of the play. Maybe this is what Shakespeare intended, or at least allowed for. But the unfeelingness of the Duke's conduct is inescapable. And Shakespeare must have been aware of that too. The Duke's treatment of Isabella stems directly from that cast of mind in which the importance of the grand design and the struggle for the greater good require a lack of responsiveness and even justify the infliction of temporary suffering. If you begin by manipulating people, even for their own presumed future benefit ('To make her heavenly comforts of despair/When it is least expected' – (ll. 106–7), you end by not treating them as people at all. The awkwardness of this incident and the way the Duke dispenses justice at the end of the play hint all too plainly at a failure in human terms of a character whom, with one part of himself, Shakespeare simultaneously offers as a paragon.

The argument here is obviously similar to the one I have put forward concerning *The Tempest*. The parallels between Prospero and the Duke are close, if not exact. Both work for beneficent ends by playing God with people's lives – specifically, by constructing plays and situations in which people perform – even though the Duke exercises rather less than the total control that Prospero does. The main personality trait which they share is an aloofness and remoteness from human contact. This serves a dual, in fact contradictory, function. It is the source of the awe tinged with veneration in which they are held by the other characters in the play, an awe which in part Shakespeare intends us to share. But their aloofness and remoteness are also the source of everything that is most disquieting about their attitudes to themselves and their dealings with the other characters – their self-absorption and self-approval, coupled with an insensitivity and harshness to those whose best interests they are theoretically seeking to promote. It is odd that Shakespeare should have been so drawn to questions of whether it is possible to manipulate people into virtue and of what this process implies about the manipulator. Edgar's actions towards his father in *King Lear* have a recognisably similar admirable–repellent quality. But the treatment of these matters in *Measure for Measure* and *The Tempest* is full of unresolved tensions and contradictory affirmations. If we are to call *Measure for Measure* a problem play, we must call *The Tempest* one too.

Coriolanus

Coriolanus is a particularly tightly knit play. It may lack something of the amplitude and metaphysical resonance of the other tragedies; but limitation implies concentration, and throughout its length our attention is directed unblinkingly to its two major concerns: Coriolanus and Rome. The fact that Coriolanus himself is very largely defined in terms of Rome and Roman values has caused the play to be regarded as the last and greatest of the histories. This is perhaps arguable. What has rarely been disputed is the claim that the play is an artistic success. For this reason alone it is a useful work on which to test the general view of Shakespeare's art that I have been putting forward.

To state my own view briefly, *Coriolanus*, for all its concentration, seems to me to be far from a seamless web. The first three acts are complex yet remarkably unified. That in fact is the problem. Scenes of rapid action, intense debate and public tumult take Coriolanus from being the acclaimed hero of Rome to a humiliating banishment. In the remainder of the play Shakespeare continued to follow North's Plutarch, a copy of which he seems at times to have had open by him as he wrote. That merely provided narrative continuity and an inevitable conclusion to work towards in Coriolanus's death. It did not solve the problem of what relation the second half of the play was to bear to the first, both structurally and in regard to the portrayal of the hero. I shall argue later that Shakespeare, characteristically, seems to have entertained divergent possibilities on both matters.

The first three acts are overwhelmingly political. However much the figure of Coriolanus himself commands our attention, he serves to bring the question of Rome into an almost equal prominence. His strongest personal relationship, that with his mother, is presented in terms of her

effect on his political attitudes and actions. The only hint of a private
self is conveyed through his wife, Virgilia, who remains 'My gracious
silence' (II i 166), embodying a world of feeling which never finds full
expression in the play. Coriolanus is the means by which Rome achieves
political definition, both through what he does and through his forceful
articulation of the issues confronting it. He insists on the necessity of
making a conscious choice between the two conceptions of Rome that
are struggling for dominance in the first part of the play. His downfall
signifies not only the collapse of what he stands for but also the
impotence of his political ideals when asserted in the face of intractable
realities.

The realities are that at the beginning of the play Rome is unable to
cope with the disruptive forces working within it. The plebeians are
rioting from hunger, and the patricians seem scarcely to know what to
do. There is an ironical appropriateness in Menenius's fable portraying
the patricians as the belly of Rome (a passive member, unable to direct
what happens to the body or to take the initiative) and not as her head;
the edifice of patrician authority is collapsing almost at a touch. The
common people, as Coriolanus disgustedly reports in the first scene,
have just had tribunes appointed to represent them, and through them
the mob is preparing to exercise a power it never knew it possessed. The
corn that was withheld at the beginning of the play is, we learn later,
distributed free to prevent further rioting. The patricians have no plan
or strategy; they make concessions on an *ad hoc* basis less out of concern
for the common people than as a means of retaining what limited
control they can over the situation. Coriolanus is predictably in no
doubt about what should be done:

> Would the nobility lay aside their ruth
> And let me use my sword, I'd make a quarry
> With thousands of these quarter'd slaves, as high
> As I could prick my lance.   (I i 195–8)

Grotesque though they sound, Coriolanus's proposals for the suppression of discontent are to him a logical expression of his belief in patrician
authority; and he, far more than his fellow patricians, can see the
implications of their failure to act decisively:

> O good but most unwise patricians! Why,

> You grave but reckless senators, have you thus
> Given Hydra here to choose an officer
> That with his peremptory 'shall', being but
> The horn and noise o' th' monster's, wants not spirit
> To say he'll turn your current in a ditch,
> And make your channel his? If he have power,
> Then vail your ignorance; if none, awake
> Your dangerous lenity. If you are learn'd,
> Be not as common fools; if you are not,
> Let them have cushions by you. . . . By Jove himself,
> It makes the consuls base; and my soul aches
> To know, when two authorities are up,
> Neither supreme, how soon confusion
> May enter 'twixt the gap of both and take
> The one by th' other.   (III i 91–101, 107–12)

The ideal which Coriolanus upholds here, of patrician authority as the guardian of order in Rome, is neither ignoble nor dishonourable; it is something in which he passionately believes – unlike his fellow patricians, who seem solely concerned with making pragmatic adjustments. Furthermore, the logic behind his analysis of what is happening to Rome is, on its own terms, irrefutable: where there is no legitimate power, confusion reigns. No one bothers to argue with him. Cominius can only reply to the speech just quoted with a muttered, 'Well, on to th' market place' (l. 112). The only argument to be made against Coriolanus is that the Rome in which he believes exists nowhere outside his imagination. From Volumnia downwards the patricians favour mixing 'Honour and policy' (III ii 42), using cajolery and flattery on the mob if that is the only way to appease them. The patricians' prevailing attitude is summed up in Menenius's words, 'This must be patch'd/ With cloth of any colour' (III i 252–3). The tragic paradox of the first part of the play is that Coriolanus, for all his lonely integrity, is wrong – since his principles amount in practice to the most brutal oppression – and that the patricians, shuffling temporisers though they may be, are right. Everything Coriolanus says and does is inflammatory and can only lead Rome to the very chaos which he deplores. The patricians' 'ruth', which to Coriolanus constitutes mere weakness, is the positive aspect of their willingness to compromise and adjust. Coriolanus's presence makes any such compromise impossible; and in a massive convulsion Rome finally expels, as an act of unconscious but necessary self-preservation, the man who was her greatest servant and her greatest threat.

The part of the tribunes, Sicinius and Brutus, in all this has received much criticism, not all of it justified. They are a self-interested pair of place-seekers, but their one significant intervention in the events of the first part of the play – inducing the common people to withdraw their assent to Coriolanus's consulship – showed a proper sense of responsibility to the people they were supposed to represent. In their view the plebeians in giving their voices to Coriolanus had acted out of 'childish friendliness' (ii iii 172). True indeed (to Coriolanus's 'Well then, I pray, your price o' th' consulship?', the First Citizen responds, 'The price is to ask it kindly' – ll. 72–3.) Brutus's conclusion, 'They have chose a consul that will from them take/Their liberties' (ll. 211–12), is simply a statement of fact. Who can blame the plebeians if, on better advice, they change their minds? They can hardly be expected to vote for their own political suicide – and, given Coriolanus's known views on the distribution of corn, more than just political suicide may be involved. Certainly Brutus and Sicinius do their rabble-rousing best to engineer the final furious confrontation between the mob and Coriolanus, but, the man being what he is, who can doubt that it would have come about sooner or later? And, when he is gone, there is no reason to question the sincerity of Sicinius's words in that rather sardonically presented idyll just before the news of Coriolanus's return:

> This is a happier and more comely time
> Than when these fellows ran about the streets
> Crying confusion.   (iv vi 27–9)

The sense of dramatic inevitability which was so marked in the first three acts is lacking in the remaining two. Although Shakespeare naturally needs to relax the tension after the high drama of Coriolanus's banishment, there is something unsatisfactory and even forced about the way the play picks itself up into life again. The short scene immediately after his departure presents an oddly diminished and even undignified Volumnia – less of the Roman matron than the Roman fishwife – and the back-pedalling by the tribunes coupled by the efforts of Menenius to shut her up give the scene a flavour of the comedy of social embarrassment. The scene that follows between a Volscian and a Roman traitor takes some fifty lines to communicate information we already know, and is redundant except in so far as the motif of treachery is meant in some obscure way to throw light on Coriolanus himself. For at this point in the play he has undoubtedly become a somewhat puzzling figure. Virtually the last words we hear from him before he goes are:

> While I remain above ground you shall
> Hear from me still, and never of me aught
> But what is like me formerly.   (IV i 51–3)

The promise is not kept. Menenius tells us a few scenes later that his wife and mother hear nothing from him. The reason, as they are all shortly to find out, is that the pillar of Rome has become the servant of the Volsci. Why? One would expect his only soliloquy in the play, coming as it does at this point, to clarify his change of allegiance. But after a turgid preamble Coriolanus talks only in general terms about 'fellest foes' becoming 'dear friends' over 'Some trick not worth an egg' (IV iv 12–26). If that is meant to apply to himself and Aufidius, it suggests that his quarrel with Rome was over the most trivial of issues. If it is not, it becomes a piece of shallow and irrelevant cynicism. Either way we are no nearer understanding his change of heart.

The play narrows its focus in the last two acts; and, although a theatrical power is generated at least equivalent to that in the first three, it is of a different kind. For the Romans – and that means for us too – there is only one question that exercises them as Coriolanus and the Volsci draw closer: will he in the end destroy Rome? Although a compelling-enough question, it is clearly different from the theoretical and practical seminar on the legitimacy of political power and the nature of political rights and responsibilities, of which much of the first half of the play had consisted.

The last two acts also manage to blur the extent of Coriolanus's own responsibility for his banishment by assiduously promoting the myth of Roman ingratitude. In the speech announcing himself to Aufidius Coriolanus refers to 'the drops of blood/Shed for my *thankless* country' (IV v 69–70), a view then endorsed by Aufidius, who talks about 'pouring war/Into the bowels of *ungrateful* Rome' (ll. 129–30). This is taken up on all sides. Even the patricians accept the justice of the charge. One can see why Shakespeare wants to create the impression of Rome's ingratitude. Without it Coriolanus's actions would seem those of a monster for whom the audience could feel nothing but loathing; he would also be so far beyond the reach of any ordinary human feeling

that his eventual decision to spare Rome would be incomprehensible.
The impression is nevertheless a travesty of the truth. Far from being
ungrateful to Coriolanus, Rome in the first three acts had been falling
over itself in its gratitude. Cominius insists on the necessity for it; so does
Menenius; so does the Second Officer in Act II scene ii; and so does the
Third Citizen:

> FIRST CITIZEN   Once, if he do require our voices, we ought not to
> deny him.
> SECOND CITIZEN   We may, sir, if we will.
> THIRD CITIZEN   We have power in ourselves to do it, but it is a
> power that we have no power to do; for if he show us his wounds
> and tell us his deeds, we are to put our tongues into those wounds
> and speak for them; so, if he tell us his noble deeds, we must also
> tell him our noble acceptance of them. Ingratitude is monstrous,
> and for the multitude to be ingrateful were to make a monster of
> the multitude; of the which we being members should bring
> ourselves to be monstrous members.   (II iii 1–12)

This speech, in its slow earnest way, makes clear that the ritual of the
gown of humility need not be an empty or cynical charade when
gratitude is allowed to be an expression of that mutuality which binds a
community together. Coriolanus, in rejecting gratitude – from whatever quarter – also rejects what it represents. To accept gratitude is to
accept human contact – and that is something that Coriolanus, an
isolated figure throughout the play, is unable to do. To his fellow
patricians he responds with embarrassed blushes and silence; to the
plebeians with angry contempt. Of neither group can it be said that
they were lacking in gratitude to Coriolanus for his services to Rome.
The truth is that he made their expression of that gratitude impossible.
In this respect the last two acts represent not only a simplification but
also a distortion of the three that preceded them.

His isolation makes him a poignant figure – fleetingly expressed in
that comparison of himself to 'a lonely dragon, that his fen/Makes
fear'd and talk'd of more than seen' (IV i 30–1). It also makes him an
enigmatic one. The main features of his personality are clear enough:
his dedication to the martial ideal of Rome; his sense of the honour and
authority of the patrician class to which he belongs; his courage, pride
and wrath; and his dependence on his mother. He has little instinct for
self-examination and little insight into his more compulsive drives; for

instance, that 'he seeks [the plebeians'] hate with greater devotion than they can render it him' (II ii 17–18). The very climax of the play–the moment when, despite everything he had repeatedly affirmed, he decides to spare Rome – is also the most enigmatic.

Perhaps it is wrong to call the moment enigmatic. It is open to two distinct but contradictory interpretations. In the light of which interpretation one chooses the structure of the play is transformed, and so too is one's view of the nature of the play Shakespeare is writing. The crucial question is: what is it that in the end makes Coriolanus relent?

One answer is that he is bound to his mother by ties which he is unable to break, and when she pleads with him he has no choice but to submit. It is her influence that is decisive here, just as it was in the first half of the play in persuading him to return and present himself a second time in the gown of humility. Significantly, on both occasions it is not her pleading but her exhausted capitulation to his intransigence that makes Coriolanus finally give way. 'Do as thou list', she says the first time (III ii 128), 'Come let us go' the second (v iii 177); and in that moment his resistance crumbles. It is as if her offer of freedom to do as *he* chooses constitutes in his eyes a symbolic rejection, and it is more than he can bear. On this view the play's structure is one of cyclic repetition. In both parts Coriolanus demonstrates his humiliating dependence on his mother; he is on the first occasion persuaded to a course to which he is totally opposed, on the second dissuaded from a course to which he is irrevocably committed. Both parts of the play enact a descent in Coriolanus's fortunes, his initial acclamation in Rome leading to banishment and his corresponding acclamation in Antium leading to his death.

The psychological origins of this structure lie not only in his ties to Volumnia but also in another aspect of his personality which is hinted at when she tells him that the Senate is now prepared to make him a consul. He replies,

> Know, good mother,
> I had rather be their servant in my way
> Than sway with them in theirs.   (II i 192–4)

In both Rome and Antium Coriolanus claimed to be the loyal and humble servant of its interests. But a sense of his own desert went hand with hand with the exercise of a natural supremacy that was both effortless and quite unconscious of itself. Being 'their servant in my way' meant in practice being utterly heedless or contemptuous of others. Through his very 'sovereignty of nature' (IV vii 35) he provoked first the fear and anger of the Roman mob, later the jealousy of Aufidius; the one caused his banishment, the other his death. The play's tragedy is of a man of extraordinary stature who had neither wish nor instinct to take his place within the confines of a larger community, preferring instead to dictate a place for himself as the state's indispensable servant. Unconscious of the contradictions between what he professed and what he practised, unconscious also of the degree of his dependence on his mother, he could do nothing about either. Lacking the capacity for self-knowledge, he lacked the capacity for change. And so the play's structural design is one in which history massively repeats itself.

The other interpretation of the play is that history does not repeat itself. At the end Coriolanus achieves a belated victory over himself, and he spares Rome out of newly awakened feelings of compassion and love. His transformation begins with the arrival from Rome of his mother, wife and child; and their joint presence works powerfully on him even before Volumnia has said a word:

> My wife comes foremost, then the honour'd mould
> Wherein this trunk was fram'd, and in her hand
> The grandchild to her blood. But out, affection!
> All bond and privilege of nature, break!
> Let it be virtuous to be obstinate.
> What is that curtsy worth? or those doves' eyes,
> Which can make gods forsworn? I melt, and am not
> Of stronger earth than others. My mother bows,
> As if Olympus to a molehill should
> In supplication nod; and my young boy
> Hath an aspect of intercession which
> Great nature cries 'Deny not'.   (v iii 22–33)

Although the inner struggle is not easily resolved, the influence on Coriolanus of his wife and child seems to be at least as strong as that of his mother. They say little compared with Volumnia, but their brief speeches coming at the end of hers draw from him a tone almost of desperation:

> Not of a woman's tenderness to be
> Requires nor child's nor woman's face to see.
> I have sat too long.   (ll. 129–31)

The focal point for both interpretations of Coriolanus's change of heart is the moment of silently holding his mother by the hand and the words that follow:

> O mother, mother!
> What have you done? Behold, the heavens do ope,
> The gods look down, and this unnatural scene
> They laugh at. O my mother, mother! O!
> You have won a happy victory to Rome;
> But for your son – believe it, O, believe it! –
> Most dangerously you have with him prevail'd,
> If not most mortal to him. But let it come.   (ll. 182–9)

Part of what makes this speech so arresting is that it is, in almost a literal sense, a moment of vision: 'Behold, the heavens do ope, / The gods look down, and this unnatural scene/They laugh at.' This reference to the gods is virtually the only one in the play with real imaginative force. Its sense of a larger cosmic perspective on the absurdities of human life represents a partial dawning of light for Coriolanus, as he starts to realise how powerful are the links that bind him to his mother and of how fatal they will now prove. There is no calculation about how his decision will be accepted by the Volsci, though the moment of insight is accompanied by a premonition of his death. 'But let it come.' It is difficult to capture the extraordinary quality of this speech, its paradoxical blend of joyfulness, despair and utter absurdity – a rising joy that he has been able to tap a deep stream of natural feeling, of spontaneous affection, that had been dammed up for so long; a despair that his awakening has come too late, that the effect of it will be to destroy him; and an over-riding sense of cosmic absurdity in the reversal of roles whereby a mother kneels to her son, and from that position Volumnia manipulates him as effectively as she did once before, so that the most momentous decision of his life may not in fact have been truly his decision at all.

The total effect of this speech cannot be simply absorbed into one or other of the two mutually exclusive conceptions of Coriolanus that the play offers, since (like the corresponding moment at the end of *The Tempest*) it can be experienced consistently with both. Whatever Shakespeare's original intentions with this play may have been, the speech expresses a Coriolanus who both does and does not manage to transcend himself, who is and is not the same man he was at the beginning.

It has to be added, though, that this moment of insight is fleeting and temporary. The play does not end here. It ends with his death in Corioli, where he returns as confident of his merit as ever and with his old self-blindness which allows him to claim to the Volscian lords that he is 'still subsisting / Under your great command' (v vi 73–4). The circumstances of his death – Aufidius's taunt 'thou boy of tears' (l. 101), the squalid and unheroic nature of the killing, the spectacle of Aufidius standing on his dead body – are a grimly fitting end for the first Coriolanus, a man of courage and nobility who was nevertheless grossly flawed and incapable of growth or change. But the play has two endings – in Rome as well as Corioli – and in Rome the relief and rejoicing at their deliverance bear witness to another Coriolanus who had achieved a belated victory over himself, who for the first and only time in the play had felt and responded to the promptings of compassion and love. The victory may have been temporary. It was none the less real for that.

6 Conclusion

The previous chapters have had two aims: to shed light on the plays being discussed and to assess the kind of help to be had from some of the major critical approaches. Underlying both aims has been the attempt to discover the source of Shakespeare's seeming inexhaustibility. It is time now to draw together the threads of these lines of investigation.

I

Different critics embody different approaches. The nature of the approach depends on what each critic brings to Shakespeare and what aspects of the plays he is trying to illuminate. Most approaches originate in the desire to give concentrated attention to an aspect of the plays which has been wholly or partially ignored. At least in principle one approach ought to complement another, even when, as is bound to happen, the same part of a play is discussed from two or more points of view. It should be possible to study a Shakespeare play with reference to the dramatic milieu out of which it grew, the current ideas which in one form or other helped to shape it, the characters, the imagery, the structure, and so on, and thereby establish a sense of the whole. Whatever the theoretical feasibility, in practice matters are not that simple. The snag lies in the natural human tendency for critics to claim more for their particular approach than it really warrants. A critic may consider that his approach does more than illuminate an aspect of a play; it is the key to that play's essential meaning – or even to Shakespeare as a whole.

Something of the sort happened in the 1930s when a group of critics felt that the plot–character–motive approach had gone too far, and an attempt was made to sweep it away in favour of a new emphasis on language and imagery: the play as dramatic poem. The revolution, if that is the right word, was one from which criticism has undoubtedly benefited. All the same, it eventually became clear that the new approach was capable of creating its own excesses, which had to be guarded against in their turn. To view a play and its imagery in spatial terms was to ignore the fact that a play is experienced over a period of time, and that our response to it does not permit, except very artificially, movement back and forth across its surface picking up images as we go; such collecting of images was sometimes done mechanically, ascribing to them a uniform importance and failing to discriminate between the genuinely significant and the merely peripheral; the approach could also lead to the unspoken assumption that Shakespeare's plays were art-works concerned with imagery, language and verbal texture for their own sake rather than for the purpose of illuminating and deepening the portrayal of specific human predicaments. It is now possible once again to discuss character without having to be brash or apologetic about it, and as a result we seem to have returned, though with enlarged understanding, to the main stream of Shakespeare criticism. The need for criticism to take account of the realities of stage performance has been increasingly emphasised in recent years; in its belief that the plays' essential life is not in the words on the page but in the words spoken by actors before an audience this approach represents part of the continuing reaction against the over-exclusive emphasis in the 1930s on Shakespeare's language.

Besides being prone to claim more for their approach than it really warrants, critics are likely to be guilty of selectivity, compression and omission in their treatment of the evidence. In a sense this is inevitable; it can be said with some truth that the only complete statement about a play is the play itself. But the critic's approach can render him blind or unsympathetic to those aspects which do not happen to fit his thesis. Until fairly recently, for example, criticism of *The Winter's Tale* had very little to say about the presence of Autolycus. He is funny of course, but apart from that what is he actually doing there? The crucial fact is that he *is* there – very prominently too in the fourth act – and, if he fails to fit neatly into a view of the play as a myth of Christian redemption, then so much the worse for that line of interpretation – in so far as it claims to give a comprehensive account.

There is practically no approach, however unorthodox, which is not capable of revealing something new and unexpected about a play. Equally, there is none, however indispensable, which is not capable of misdirecting us in some way or other. Each of the approaches looked at in the earlier chapters has its own distinctive way of going wrong. Historical criticism can impose upon a play a rigid ideological framework into which the evidence of the play is thrust. Allegorical criticism can detect in a play a system of ideas for which there is only the most vestigial evidence, or even none at all. Thematic criticism can draw into sharp and over-simple focus something the play leaves open and unresolved. And character criticism can go beyond the evidence of what is there and create extensive off-stage lives for Shakespeare's dramatic characters.

This seems to point to the incontestable, if unexciting, conclusion that an approach is as good or bad as the critic who employs it. But are all approaches equal? Are some more valuable, more important, more central, than others? If so, which ones?

Common sense indicates there must be some kind of pecking-order. Marxist criticism has not figured at all in the preceding pages, partly because there is much less of it than of other kinds of criticism, partly – what amounts to the same thing – because the plays do not seem greatly to encourage this approach. (The paradox is that, the more fully responsive it is to what the plays contain, the less will its results bear an unmistakably Marxist stamp.) Allegorical criticism too, as we have seen, does not take us very far with *The Tempest*, and it is even less useful with the other plays. Shakespeare's plays then appear to invite certain approaches and put up a resistance to others. This suggests, as a rule of thumb, that the most important approaches are those which have produced the greatest bulk of critical writing. Using such a test we would have to grant a special place to character criticism, particularly if, as I think we should, we extend its range beyond that of individual character studies.[1] Our involvement in a Shakespeare play should start – does start – with a response to the richness, variety, subtlety, intelligence and power of its portrayal of human experience.

Because, however, a play is a work of art and not a direct transcription from life, we recognise – more or less consciously – something of the way in which it has been shaped. To enable us to understand the work fully we need those approaches which concern themselves with language, structure, sources and all the manifold influences that bear upon its creation. All I would add, to echo what I have said already, is that the approach through, say, a play's literary analogues is not a substitute for discussion of the play's more immediate effects. Nor can it take precedence over them. It can serve

only to reinforce, amplify, heighten or qualify what is mediated much
more directly through character and action.

II

I am talking here in general terms. Individual plays differ, and each one
should be allowed to determine the way in which it can be most usefully
approached and discussed. We must avoid, knowingly at least,
thrusting the play into a straitjacket of our own making. Ideally, no
doubt, we should be free of all limiting assumptions and preconceptions.
Some nevertheless, are inevitable. We cannot transform ourselves into a
tabula rasa, nor is it desirable we should try. We cannot encounter the
play without some mental framework or set of assumptions into which
our experience of it will fit, but any such framework runs the risk of
constricting and distorting the play. In acknowledging the fact, it would
seem an appropriate moment for me now to sum up the assumptions
about Shakespeare on which the present study has been based.

The minimum claim I would make (I cannot imagine anyone
wanting to disagree with it) is that the plays, complex as they are, were
not unplanned. When Shakespeare put pen to paper he had at least a
rough idea where he was going. The likelihood is that he had
considerably more than this; his plays show evidence of much prior
thought and planning. Though the question of how much planning is
unanswerable in precise terms, each play has its own bone-structure
which reveals something about the original design. But, whatever
Shakespeare had in mind when he started a particular play, however
complex or simple may have been the original conception, the finished
work usually suggests that an increase has taken place in its dramatic
range and depth. Although much of the play may have been planned in
advance, not everything in it could have been – hence the feeling of
amplitude and experiential fullness that is a characteristic part of our
response to Shakespeare. His genius was exploratory; he had an
unparalleled capacity for sensing possibilities and potentialities in his
material, some of them consistent with each other, some of them not. I
have tried to show that in some plays Shakespeare had more than one
view of the significance and implications of his material. At one level he
gave himself wholly to what he was working with, and followed where
his imagination led. But at another level he remained the conscious
artist aware of the need to organise, to restrain the fertility of his

invention, to redirect it perhaps back into original channels as the end of the play approached, to harmonise his increasingly complex material. Shakespeare's art was a technique of inclusion, whereby a supremely creative imagination was balanced by equally remarkable powers of artistic organisation. That there should be a tension between them was inevitable. The structure of the plays, however flexible, was bound to reflect the twin impulses towards increasing simplicity and increasing complexity – the drive towards neatness, pointedness, the possibility of explicit summary constantly subverted by that larger awareness of multiplicity, alternative points of view, deeper implications, carried even to the point of inconsistency and internal contradiction. All Shakespeare's plays are experimental. Whatever their subject-matter, all are involved in tackling with varying degrees of success the same recurring artistic problem.

At the beginning of this study I proposed, no doubt rashly, to try to deal with the problem of relativism in Shakespeare criticism. The foregoing description of what I take to be the underlying structure of the plays is not susceptible of proof. I hope nevertheless that it sheds some light on the way they work, and that it also helps to explain both why critics disagree so much about the plays and why Shakespeare has been – and will continue to be – so inexhaustible. If the arguments in the previous part of the book do not seem convincing on their own, there is now one further consideration to be advanced in their favour: that is, their unoriginality.

III

The view of Shakespeare offered here derives from the central tradition of Shakespeare criticism. A few representative examples will serve to indicate what that tradition is:

> as he was a happie imitator of Nature, [Shakespeare] was a most gentle expresser of it.   (Heminge and Condell)

> Hee . . . had an excellent *Phantsie*; brave notions, and gentle expressions: wherein hee flow'd with that facility, that sometime it was necessary he should be stop'd.   (Jonson)

> he was the man who of all Modern, and perhaps Ancient Poets, had

the largest and most comprehensive soul. All the Images of Nature
were still present to him.   (Dryden)

His *Characters* are so much Nature her self, that 'tis a sort of injury to
call them by so distant a name as Copies of her.   (Pope)

Shakespeare's plays are not in the rigorous or critical sense either
tragedies or comedies, but compositions of a distinct kind; exhibiting
the real state of sublunary nature, which partakes of good and evil,
joy and sorrow, mingled with endless variety of proportion and
innumerable modes of combination; and expressing the course of the
world, in which the loss of one is the gain of another; in which, at the
same time, the reveller is hasting to his wine, and the mourner
burying his friend.   (Johnson)[2]

These quotations from the seventeenth and eighteenth centuries with
their praise of his generous inclusiveness indicate the core of the
tradition: Shakespeare the poet of Nature, whose plays are a comprehensive mirror of life.

In the nineteenth century this tradition developed along two
seemingly incompatible lines. The first one invoked a conception of
Shakespeare as the God-like creator of a world from which his own
thoughts, feelings, personality and beliefs were totally absent, Shakespeare as *deus absconditus* in fact. This view can be traced back to
Coleridge and Hazlitt:

Shakespeare's poetry is characterless; that is, it does not reflect the
individual Shakespeare. . . . The body and substance of his works
came out of the unfathomable depths of his own oceanic
mind.   (Coleridge)

He was nothing in himself, but he was all that others were, or that
they could become. He not only had in himself the germs of every
faculty and feeling, but he could follow them by anticipation,
intuitively, into all their conceivable ramifications, through every
change of fortune or conflict of passion, or turn of thought.

(Hazlitt)[3]

Later in the century John Ruskin referred to Shakespeare in similar
terms:

It was necessary that he should lean *no* way; that he should contemplate, with absolute equality of judgement, the life of the court, cloister, and tavern, and be able to sympathise so completely with all creatures as to deprive himself, together with his personal identity, even of his conscience, as he cast himself into their hearts.[4]

The tradition is still detectable in the twentieth century, as in this comment by Edmund Wilson: 'Shakespeare expands himself, breeds his cells as organic beings, till he has so lost himself in the world he has made that we can hardly recompose his personality.'[5]

At the same time the nineteenth century, more specifically the Romantic movement, gave birth to an entirely opposed tradition. If all good poetry was, as Wordsworth claimed, 'the spontaneous overflow of powerful feelings', then it followed that in some form Shakespeare expressed himself through his writings, and his personality, thoughts and feelings could be inferred from the plays. Edward Dowden tried to trace 'the growth of his intellect and character from. youth to full maturity',[6] a process involving four stages, 'In the workshop', 'In the world', 'Out of the depths' and 'On the heights'. This line of criticism received a spirited rebuttal from C. J. Sisson in 'The Mythical Sorrows of Shakespeare'.[7] It has nevertheless shown a remarkable capacity for survival. Caroline Spurgeon claimed that the plays tell us, among other things, that he was nimble and deft with his hands, a keen athlete, and particularly good at bowls.[8] With greater literary tact L. C. Knights confined *Some Shakespearean Themes* to questions of the dramatist's beliefs rather than his personality, and argued that in the plays Shakespeare was exploring matters of general as well as personal concern.

Despite the apparent incompatibility of the two traditions – Shakespeare as either absent from or present in what he writes – they clearly answer strongly to so many people's feelings about the plays that there is no question of simply rejecting one in favour of the other. It is more profitable to look for whatever it is in Shakespeare that gave rise to both traditions – the Shakespeare, that is to say, who is both present in *and* absent from his works. Such a paradoxical conception is contained in a celebrated formulation about the nature of his art, on which the whole of this study has been an extended commentary. I refer to Keats's definition of Negative Capability:

it struck me what quality went to form a man of achievement, especially in literature, and which Shakespeare possessed so enormously – I mean *Negative Capability*, that is, when a man is capable of being in uncertainties, mysteries, doubts without any irritable reaching after fact and reason.[9]

Keats here, it seems to me, simultaneously affirms both the personally expressive and the impersonal aspects of Shakespeare, the Shakespeare who both is and is not present in his work. Keats catches the essence of a dramatist who is fully engaged in his material, open and responsive to its implications, and who for that very reason is reluctant to impose a simplifying pattern upon it. It is Shakespeare's reticence about resolving the 'uncertainties, mysteries, doubts' that produces the characteristically open-ended, even contradictory, quality of so many of the plays.

IV

Keats's definition of Negative Capability I find enormously congenial, subject only to a few qualifications. I would want to claim for Shakespeare a greater degree of conscious artistic control over his work than Keats seems to imply. What varies is the extent to which Shakespeare's presence is overtly detectable. Sometimes we do sense an 'irritable reaching after fact and reason'. We are aware of an intrusiveness – a promising line of development cut off here, a conclusion forced somewhat against the grain of the preceding action there. Shakespeare has to be true to the complexity of his chosen subject-matter; he also has to avoid creating something that becomes humanly and artistically chaotic. The matter *is* one of deep personal concern to Shakespeare; it is also beyond personality. Both the desire for harmony and the difficulty, if not impossibility, of achieving it make equal and opposite demands on him. D. H. Lawrence wrote that 'Thought is a man in his wholeness wholly attending.'[10] For Shakespeare wholeness was somehow bound up with the attempt to attend wholly to the promptings of his creativity, of what Coleridge called his 'oceanic mind'.

Keats's stress on 'uncertainties, mysteries, doubts' also tends to minimise the extent to which 'fact and reason' are already there as an informing presence in the structure of the plays. The larger context of Shakespeare's dramatic world is the moral and spiritual beliefs of his contemporaries. For Shakespeare the basic structure was conveyed by a belief in the orderly nature of society and human relations symbolised by the concept of Degree and what it implied in terms of human rights and responsibilities. The notion of Degree was still a datum of his society; it no longer had the intellectually constricting effect of a rigid system, and yet neither had New Philosophy nor political republicanism completely called it in doubt. It was something which for Shakespeare existed in flawed actuality and in ideal. If God represented the peak of this hierarchical ordering – and, what is more important, its theoretical justification and source of strength – then, in some sense, if God did not exist it would be necessary to invent Him. Equally, God served to provide that tension between the actual and the ideal which stretched the tragedies to their fullest intensity. Shakespeare's personal religious beliefs are hardly discernible from the plays. The diffused influence of Christianity permeates the plays in a way that is inevitable for someone standing, as he did, at the centre of his age, but that is all. Not merely do they contain nothing doctrinal; they suggest a Shakespeare committed to this world in a way that made him disinclined to agonise over the next. The range and fineness of his response to his age are such that one has indeed, fleetingly, the awed sensation of participating in the consciousness not of a single individual but of a culture at a particular time in its history.

The advances in scholarship which have revealed how unhistorical is the monolithic view of Shakespeare's age enshrined in Tillyard's *The Elizabethan World Picture* provide a belated justification for Keats's way of looking at Shakespeare and for the variation of it which I have been putting forward. They also make it possible to dispose of the objection that the views expressed here derive from a false contemporaneity. Everything I have written has drawn implicitly and explicitly on notions of ambiguity, ambivalence and paradox, terms which have a suspiciously modern ring: is this not a case of the Age of Uncertainty projecting its own uncertainties onto Shakespeare and hearing as a result not Shakespeare's voice but an echo of its own? In some hypothetically more unified and self-confident age than ours may not all this insistence on ambiguity seem an aberration which reveals more about the twentieth century than it does about Shakespeare? The answer to such questions is that, if a responsiveness to possible ambiguity in Shakespeare turns out to throw light on the plays, it is because the ambiguity is there. Keats felt its presence over a hundred and fifty years ago. It is true of course that with an art as rich and wide-ranging as Shakespeare's there is a tendency for any age – or any individual – to take from the plays what it finds most congenial and to leave what is not. No doubt too Shakespeare is sufficiently Protean to provide evidence in support of a diversity of views, even contradictory ones. But it is this very Protean quality that most calls out for explanation.

V

In recent years critics have paid an increasing attention to this aspect of Shakespeare's work – a fact which reinforces my point about the relative unoriginality of the views on which the present study is based. A few quotations will indicate the form this interest in Shakespeare has been taking. The first is Ernest Schanzer's well-known definition of a problem play.

> The definition of the Shakespearian problem play which I therefore suggest is: 'A play in which we find a concern with a moral problem which is central to it, presented in such a manner that we are unsure of our moral bearings, so that uncertain and divided responses to it in the minds of the audience are possible or even probable'.[11]

> Since a mixed or divided response may be associated too exclusively with a Shakespearian 'problem play', Rossiter's essay on ambivalence or 'doubleness of feeling' in the histories should be pondered carefully. There are good reasons, I think, for not appropriating the mixed response to a single genre – for regarding it, rather, as related to Shakespeare's way of looking at character, and as equally suited to comedy, history and tragedy. And, as I shall try to show, the tragic hero no less than the villain calls forth a mixed response, and will be improperly sentimentalised if we gloss over his savage and unnatural thoughts and deeds.[12]

> Throughout his life, then, Shakespeare probed and experimented in a determined effort to expand the limits of [tragedy]. And central to this exploration was the development of an effective perspective through which to provoke the spectators to share the genuine ambivalence of the tragic experience. . . . Based on the assumption that reality is more complex when viewed from two or more points of

view, this tragic perspective holds the emotions of the spectators in tension, simultaneously arousing sympathy for and censure upon the protagonist.[13]

Schanzer's original point, however, went beyond saying that the characters invoke a more complex response than simple endorsement or rejection. He claimed there is an ambivalence in the values informing some of Shakespeare's plays, and that this leads us into making uncertain or mutually irreconcilable judgements. This assertion has been taken up and its application widened to include more than just the problem plays.

> Shakespeare maintains amid the obvious variety of his work a strikingly consistent approach to the world he imitates. . . . Shakespeare tends to structure his imitations in terms of a pair of polar opposites – reason and passion in Hamlet, for instance, or reason and faith, reason and love, reason and imagination; *Realpolitik* and the traditional social order, *Realpolitik* and political idealism; hedonism and responsibility, the world and the transcendent, life and death, justice and mercy. Generally the opposition is rather between two complexes of related elements than simply between two single ideals. Always the dramatic structure sets up the opposed elements as equally valid, equally desirable, and equally destructive, so that the choice that the play forces the reader to make becomes impossible.[14]

> The situation in which two mutually exclusive views exert inexorable claims . . . is an important aspect of tragic experience in the other mature tragedies as well. Final intellectual resolution is impossible beyond the paradoxical 'And that's true too'. . . . Basically, mature Shakespearean tragedy is built around a few of the fundamental tensions generated by the conflict between opposed world-views. The issues involved do not take the form of questions, still less of theories, but rather of diametrically opposed possibilities about the nature of reality, about man's relation to the world and the cosmos, about the value of his actions and the limitations of his capabilities. The dialectical tension between those opposites permeates the thematic structure of all four plays.[15] [*Hamlet, Othello, King Lear* and *Macbeth*]

A formulation in terms of 'dialectical tension' suggests the plays are more systematically conceived than I take them to be. So far from structuring his plays in terms of polar opposites, Shakespeare seems to me to have had an abiding sense of the mysteriousness of human experience, with all that that implies about the difficulty of giving it artistic form. Philip Edwards puts the point well in suggesting a triangular relationship between unorganised experience, the intrinsic nature of things – truth – and the models of reality created by the artist:

> The endeavour of all art, surely, is to shrink this triangle until it becomes a single point, experience, art and truth becoming synonymous. But in all art the triangle remains a triangle, however much its sides and size are reduced. Experience protests that art has not netted the whole, and truth remains at a shadowy distance. The three points are permanently and inevitably separated. Witnessing an art as great as Shakespeare's, we see the triangle diminish uniquely, so that time after time we feel compelled to say that it has gone; but given an artist as honest as Shakespeare we have to acknowledge with him that art can never bring off the consummation of embracing all experience and giving it the ultimate explanation.[16]

Howard Felperin sees Shakespeare responding differently to this same challenge to give artistic form to human experience; he claims that the dramatist uses as framework for his play an older dramaturgical model which is amplified and then discarded:

> Any artist, in order to represent life, must resort to the conventions of art, and in so doing, falsify life in so far as art creates a world rival to life's. . . . Shakespeare resolves this paradox by subsuming within his work a recognizably conventional model of life, repudiating that model, and thereby creating the illusion that he uses no art at all, that he is presenting life directly. Of course what he is really presenting is a more complicated model with . . . an appeal from convention to nature. One reverend Vice of the moralities is a coward. . . . Falstaff is like this Vice; yet he is also, as Shakespeare makes equally clear, unlike this Vice in so far as he expresses a range of emotion well beyond that of an allegorical abstraction.[17]

One final example:

> What I have written is not, it seems to me, a study of Shakespeare's

Christianity or of the Christianity of Shakespeare's art. What it has turned out to be is a study of Shakespeare's negative capability. The mysteries which Shakespeare confronts in these plays remain mysteries when the plays are over and are, if anything, more profoundly disquieting than they were before his imaginative considerations of them.[18]

VI

The great merit of the notion of Negative Capability is that it directs us to an awareness of the openness of texture of Shakespeare's plays. Instead of subtly and continuously controlling our response to the plays, as some of the preceding critics suggest, Shakespeare often leaves it up to us to make what we can (or want) out of what he has written. If it is true that the plays open themselves to conflicting interpretations, it follows that some of the evidence must be capable of being taken in more than one way; it must be possible to enlist the same moment in the play in the service of mutually exclusive interpretations. Shakespeare confers on us a freedom that we are obliged to exercise. The consequence is that critics do interpret the plays differently; they are right to do so; and the 'correct' interpretation is not necessarily one of two conflicting possibilities – it is often both together.

In some of Shakespeare's plays (I hope it is clear that I am not offering a formula to be imposed mechanically on all of them) it is possible to see a moment of crucial and determining importance, coming near the end of the play, which may be properly interpreted in quite different ways; and depending on the way it is interpreted our view of the character who is speaking, and indeed the balance of the whole play, undergo a radical shift.

The first two examples of what I mean need only brief mention as they have already been discussed at some length. At the end of *The Tempest* either Prospero is converted by Ariel from revenge to forgiveness, or he merely performs what had been his consistent intention throughout. R. A. Foakes, as we have seen (pp. 95–6), takes the former view. Thomas McFarland takes the latter: 'It is perhaps the most exquisite of the many wonderful moments in the play. . . . Prospero finds his reasons not in the divine analogy he shadows forth but in his participation in mankind.'[19]

When Coriolanus relents and spares Rome, what is taking place is either a victory for love or a victory for Volumnia. On the one hand, for Wilson Knight, 'The heavens do truly open, as for the first time he realizes love's intolerant autonomy within his breast.'[20] On the other, in the view of D. J. Enright, 'Do we not rather feel that it is a victory less of love than of Volumnia's prestige and of her hardness; that the mother has had what is really the last word?'[21]

The last scene of *Measure for Measure* has several well-orchestrated climaxes, and one of the most dramatic is the moment when Isabella kneels to plead for Angelo's life:

> Most bounteous sir,
> Look, if it please you, on this man condemn'd,
> As if my brother liv'd. I partly think
> A due sincerity govern'd his deeds
> Till he did look on me; since it is so,
> Let him not die. My brother had but justice,
> In that he did the thing for which he died;
> For Angelo,
> His act did not o'ertake his bad intent,
> And must be buried but as an intent
> That perish'd by the way. Thoughts are no subjects;
> Intents but merely thoughts.   (v i 441–52)

The view one takes of this moment determines – and maybe is determined by – the view one takes of the play as a whole. Outwardly it is a gesture of mercy, but is it the real thing or a hollow mockery? The reader or spectator who has become disillusioned with the Duke and his manipulation of the various characters may well find here little to impress. The gesture costs Isabella little, and so its emotional and moral significance is slight at best. Her words may be felt as even faintly repellent.

> One's spirit recoils at hearing this girl, who had not a word to say in excuse of her brother but rather admitted the justice of his doom, now plead, with all the finesse of a seasoned attorney, on the most purely legalistic grounds for her would-be ravisher and the judicial murderer of her brother.[22]

Against this it may be argued that we are entitled to infer some residual pain at her brother's death, and at the manner of it. Her appeal for mercy rests upon her overcoming the natural impulse to revenge, and the moment of kneeling can be a real and moving act of self-transcendence, expressing a genuinely felt plea for mercy in the only terms which her nature permitted. That the moment can be staged in this way has been demonstrated by Peter Brook:

> When I once staged the play I asked Isabella, before kneeling for Angelo's life, to pause each night until she felt the audience could take it no longer – and this used to lead to a two-minute stopping of the play. The device became a voodoo pole – a silence in which all the invisible elements of the evening came together, a silence in which the abstract notion of mercy became concrete for that moment to those present.[23]

For my final example I should like to go outside the plays discussed so far and quote at length from Stanley Wells's analysis of Peter Hall's 1969 Stratford production of *Hamlet* with David Warner in the title role:

> When, some time ago, I was writing a guide to scholarship and criticism of *Hamlet*, I read within a few months a lot of writings about the play. It seemed to me then that interpretations of it tended to divide according to the view taken of one particular passage. It is part of the dialogue between Hamlet and Horatio shortly before Hamlet is to duel with Laertes, who, we know, intends to bring about Hamlet's death.
>
> HAMLET   I shall win at the odds, but thou wouldst not think how ill all's here about my heart. But it is no matter.
> HORATIO   Nay, good my lord –
> HAMLET   It is but foolery, but it is a kind of gain giving as would perhaps trouble a woman.
> HORATIO   If your mind dislike anything, obey it. I will forestall their repair hither and say you are not fit.
> HAMLET   Not a whit. We defy augury. There is a special providence in the fall of a sparrow. If it be now, 'tis not to come; if it be not to come, it will be now; if it be not now, yet it will come. The readiness is all. Since no man has aught of what he leaves, what is't to leave betimes? Let be.   (v ii 212–25)

A. C. Bradley, in 1904, had indicated two possible ways of taking the passage, while also stating his own preference. 'There is,' he says, 'a trait about which doubt is impossible, – a sense in Hamlet [after his return from England] that he is in the hands of Providence.' Citing several passages, including the one that I have quoted, he cannot believe, all the same, 'with some critics, that they indicate any material change in his general condition, or the formation of any effective resolution to fulfil the appointed duty. On the contrary, they seem to express that kind of religious resignation which, however beautiful in one aspect, really deserves the name of fatalism rather than that of faith in Providence' (*Shakespearean Tragedy* [London, 1904], pp. 144–5). This attitude recurs in later criticism. H. B. Charlton, a confessed disciple of Bradley, puts it more strongly; diagnosing in Hamlet a progressive paralysis ending in despair, he finds in him not 'the calm attainment of a higher benignity,' but 'a fatalist's surrender of his personal responsibility.' The 'sparrow' speech is 'no firm confession of trust in a benign Providence; it is merely the courage of despair' (*Shakespearian Tragedy* [Cambridge, 1949], p. 103). E. M. W. Tillyard, quoting C. S. Lewis and Middleton Murry as critics who have regarded the 'sparrow' passage as a sign of Hamlet's ultimate spiritual regeneration, argues against them. 'Quietism not religious enlightenment is the dominating note' (*Shakespeare's Problem Plays* [London, 1950], p. 17). Hamlet is not regenerate; therefore he classes it as a 'problem play'. No less damaging in 1960 was L. C. Knights, who also quotes this passage along with C. S. Lewis's expression of the point of view that Bradley had found it impossible to believe. Lewis had said that Hamlet had lost his way, and that this was 'the precise moment at which he finds it again'. Knights disagrees; Hamlet represents rather 'a corruption of consciousness' which results 'in an inability to affirm at all' (*An Approach to 'Hamlet'* [London, 1960], p. 90).

While I was citing some of these judgements on Hamlet, you may have been recalling some of Peter Hall's comments on the play and some of the reviewers' comments on Mr. Warner. Peter Hall spoke of 'a terrible fatalism' in Hamlet; Bradley had used the same word. Hall spoke of an 'apathy of the will,' which may recall Charlton's phrase 'a fatalist's surrender of his personal responsibility'. . . . . It may seem then that the Hamlet who, according to Harold Hobson, showed in the 'sparrow' speech that he 'cannot bring himself to believe that that providence extends also to him,' who had shied away from responsibility and who died on a giggle, was a logical theatrical projection of a view of the character that had begun to appear in criticism of the play at least sixty years before this production.[24]

VII

Although I am citing these comments on *Hamlet* chiefly for their relevance to my general argument, they also raise questions about the relation between theatrical interpretation and literary criticism. J. L. Styan[25] has demonstrated the way in which during this century critics and directors have moved closer together, each gaining by the contribution which the other has to make to a fuller understanding of the plays. As the convergence may help to prevent critics producing wire-drawn interpretations that could not possibly be rendered in theatrical terms, it is no doubt to be welcomed. But, as in the case of Peter Hall's *Hamlet*, directors are often critics *manqués*, and their not-unnatural desire to base a production on a coherent reading of the play entails the same risk of exaggeration and omission that critics are prone to. Uncut productions of Shakespeare are rare, and the director's blue pencil has sometimes been exercised in the same way as a critic who ignores a particular passage because it does not fit in with the argument he is developing.

Two productions by Peter Brook illustrate the way in which selective cutting can give emphasis to a director's point of view. His *King Lear* in 1962 was influenced by Jan Kott, who saw the play as expressing a mood of nihilistic despair similar to that of Beckett's *Endgame*.[26] The decision to omit the lines by Cornwall's servants showing horror and pity for the blinded Gloucester had presumably the object of creating a world even bleaker and more cruel than that in Shakespeare. In 1950 Brook had produced *Measure for Measure*, a production which, as was evident from his own words quoted earlier, placed a great emphasis on the theme of mercy and by implication on the Duke as the agent of Isabella's transformation. This conception was clearly influenced by critics such as Wilson Knight and F. R. Leavis, who had stressed the Duke's spiritual and moral authority. In order to create this effect, however, extensive pruning had to be performed on all those parts of the play which made him appear pompous, ridiculous or self-centred.[27]

It seems churlish to complain about this kind of cutting when the results are as theatrically compelling as these two productions. Nevertheless, such action has implications for any claim that the theatre is the real arbiter of the significance of Shakespeare's work. It is salutary to be reminded in this connection of the travesties of Shakespeare which the theatre has inflicted on audiences from the seventeenth century to the present day; respect for the theatre must be partly tempered by the theatre's own historical lack of respect for Shakespeare.[28] Modern productions are by and large more informed and scrupulous than those in the past, but even the most conscientious director would concede that, with or without cutting, no single theatrical interpretation can exhaust what a Shakespeare play has to offer. The Shakespearean fullness necessarily goes beyond the effects created in any single production – though most of all, it should be said, in one where the director is concerned about its intellectual coherence.

A possible way forward has been suggested by John Russell Brown. Instead of the director imposing his own interpretative stamp on the production, let the actors be set free in conditions similar to those of Shakespeare's day where rehearsal time was minimal and where theatrical effect depended on the sparks struck off by the actors themselves in their encounter with the words, with each other, and with a particular audience.

> The many different and conflicting interpretations that each of Shakespeare's major characters has been given on stage and in scholarly study, each convincing in its own context, are the most obvious indication of the chameleon qualities of Shakespeare's text. His words lie open to almost any interpretation.[29]

The 'chameleon qualities of Shakespeare's text' provide the rationale for a production based on continuous improvisation. There is a risk that it may lapse into incoherence. But it may also capture more of Shakespeare's elusive multiplicity and render it with greater freshness and life than one that is more conventionally thought out.

VIII

Although most of the preceding discussion has been directed towards individual plays, I am concerned less to gain assent to specific interpretations than to convince the reader of the usefulness to himself of the route by which they were arrived at. If it is to be called an approach, it is one which I hope is broad and flexible enough to be adapted by the reader for his own purposes in discovering further meanings – not only in these plays but also in the rest of Shakespeare's work.

I stress the point because, in looking back over this investigation into Shakespeare's art and noticing in particular those critics who have drawn attention to the ambiguity and ambivalences in Shakespeare's dramatic vision, I am struck by the gloomy thought that we may have here the beginnings of yet another 'approach to Shakespeare' to go with all the others set out in the first chapter. Critical orthodoxies establish themselves with disturbing ease. One's heart sinks at the prospect of students keeping a keen eye open for significant ambiguities, just as they were once on the look-out for recurrent images. Not so long ago Malcolm Bradbury wrote a satire on university life, *Eating People is Wrong*, in which a minor character was an English research student whose thesis topic was 'Fish Imagery in Shakespeare's Tragedies'. I have no wish to promote anything similar centred on notions of Shakespearean ambiguity.

The mechanical accumulation of ambiguities is a valueless exercise. But any way of approaching Shakespeare becomes mechanical if it is not energised by a strong imaginative response. In this context Keats's dictum about Shakespeare's Negative Capability has a special significance. Its very inexplicitness gives it an unusual power to stimulate our imaginations. In discouraging narrowness and rigidity it enlarges and enhances our response; it fosters, even though it cannot guarantee, a fuller and more intense awareness of what Shakespeare has created.

My final point is that, besides setting out to add to our understanding of Shakespeare, this study has been an attempt to demystify him. This has led me to a scepticism about one assumption on which criticism often proceeds, that of Shakespeare's artistic perfection. Such an assumption seems to me in the case of most of his plays to be unfounded. It is slightly uncomfortable to state the matter thus baldly, but the conclusion is entailed in what I have argued throughout. The myth of Shakespeare's perfection strikes me as far from beneficial in some of its effects. I am thinking here particularly of students of English who are led tacitly to believe that in his pre-eminence Shakespeare is not merely different in degree but also different in kind from all other writers. The results of this attitude, absorbed unconsciously for the most part, are to be seen in the way students often write less well on Shakespeare than on other writers, not because he is more difficult but because he seems more intimidating.

The arguments for an alternative view of Shakespeare's artistry have not, I hope, given the impression of being conducted in a spirit of subtle denigration. To say that a work is less than perfectly realised is not necessarily to place it on a lower level of achievement than one that seems flawless. Of all the plays we have looked at, the one which comes closest to a harmonious resolution of form and content is *Henry IV, Part 1*; it is certainly the greatest of the histories, but it is not for that reason necessarily a finer or a greater play than *King Lear*. Shakespeare was an experimental dramatist all his working life, testing new forms, adapting old, recognising the inevitable conflict between everything he wanted to express and the limitations of the artistic frameworks within which he had to express it. Given the nature of the undertaking, some degree of failure was to be expected. But what we experience most strongly in all his plays is not the lack of formal perfection, rather the sense of how much has been achieved. It is possible to see Shakespeare as a dramatist to be approached reverentially, whose faults, when viewed from the correct angle, will turn out not to be faults at all – a Shakespeare who never did wrong but with just cause. But the Shakespeare I have tried to describe seems to me more humanly accessible, artistically fascinating, and ultimately of greater worth.

Notes and References

Place of publication is London, unless otherwise stated.

I LITERARY CRITICISM AND SHAKESPEARE

1. The treatment of these matters is intentionally brief. Fuller and more philosophically rigorous considerations are contained in René Wellek and Austin Warren, *Theory of Literature*, 3rd edn (1966); E. D. Hirsch Jr, *Validity in Interpretation* (New Haven, Conn., and London, 1967); and John Casey, *The Language of Criticism* (1966).
2. Derek Traversi, *Shakespeare: The Last Phase* (1954) p. 268.
3. Bonamy Dobrée, '*The Tempest*', *Essays and Studies* (1952) p. 15.
4. The phrase is the title of an influential essay in W. K. Wimsatt Jr and Monroe C. Beardsley, *The Verbal Icon* (Lexington, Ky, 1954).
5. For an account of how a work can take a different direction from the one its author intended see John Fowles, *The French Lieutenant's Woman* (1969) ch. 13.
6. Kenneth Muir, *Shakespeare's Tragic Sequence* (1972) p. 12.

2 'LOVE'S LABOUR'S LOST'

1. Robert Y. Turner, *Shakespeare's Apprenticeship* (Chicago, Ill. 1974) p. 185. Cf. 'The play . . . is today generally regarded as a delicate and controlled movement towards an acceptance of reality' – Ralph Berry, 'The Words of Mercury', *Shakespeare Survey 22* (Cambridge, 1969) p. 69.
2. Harley Granville-Barker, *Prefaces to Shakespeare: First Series* (1927) pp. 14, 17. For a recent view reinforcing Granville-Barker's see J. C. Trewin, *Going to Shakespeare* (1978): 'If the acting rhythms are right, the play will dance itself into memory' (p. 73).
3. Ibid., p. 31.
4. L. E. Pearson, *Elizabethan Love Conventions* (Berkeley, Calif., 1933) p. 288.

5. John Vyvyan, *Shakespeare and Platonic Beauty* (1961) p. 66.

6. G. Wilson Knight, *The Shakespearean Tempest* (Oxford, 1940) pp. 79–80.

7. Edward Dowden, *Shakespeare: A Critical Study of His Mind and Art* (1875) pp. 62–4.

8. H. B. Charlton, *Shakespearian Comedy* (1938) pp. 271–2.

9. Ibid., p. 271.

10. M. M. Mahood, *Shakespeare's Wordplay* (1957) pp. 175–6.

11. E. M. W. Tillyard, *Shakespeare's Early Comedies* (1965) pp. 173–4.

12. Bobbyann Roesen (Anne Barton), '*Love's Labour's Lost*', *Shakespeare Quarterly*, IV (1953) 415–16.

13. Ibid., p. 416.

14. Ibid., p. 425.

15. This view of Shakespeare's structuring of the relations between the men and the women is endorsed implicitly or explicitly by many critics. See, for example, H. M. Richmond, *Shakespeare's Sexual Comedy* (Indianapolis, Ind. 1971); and William C. Carroll, *The Great Feast of Language in 'Love's Labour's Lost'* (Princeton, NJ, 1976).

16. Richard David, 'Shakespeare's Comedies and the Modern Stage', *Shakespeare Survey 4* (Cambridge, 1951) p. 132.

17. Alexander Leggatt, however, comments, 'there is something sadistic in Rosaline's attitude to Berowne' – *Shakespeare's Comedy of Love* (1974) p. 79.

18. The possibility is explored in Carroll, *The Great Feast of Language*, which sees the play as finding a reconciliation of opposites in the final songs. By contrast, John Wilders in 'The Unresolved Conflicts in *Love's Labour's Lost*', *Essays in Criticism*, XXVII (1977) 20–33, argues that the play does not encourage uncritical endorsement of any character, set of attitudes, or issue, and that our sympathies are complex and to a large extent suspended to the very end of the play.

3 'HENRY IV'

1. Lily B. Campbell, *Shakespeare's 'Histories': Mirrors of Elizabethan Policy* (San Marino, Calif., 1947) pp. 214–15. Cf. the statement that although Shakespeare 'is not primarily concerned . . . with preaching the Tudor doctrine of non-resistance . . . there can be no doubt that Shakespeare concurred in this doctrine' – Irving Ribner, *The English History Play in the Age of Shakespeare* (Princeton, NJ, 1957) pp. 180–1.

2. Ibid., p. 213.

3. E. M. W. Tillyard, *Shakespeare's History Plays* (1944) p. 277.

4. Ibid.

5. A. P. Rossiter, 'Ambivalence: The Dialectic of the Histories', in *Angel with Horns*, ed. Graham Storey (1961) p. 59.

6. Robert Ornstein, *A Kingdom for a Stage* (Cambridge, Mass., 1972) p. 4. See also his 'Historical Criticism and the Interpretation of Shakespeare', *Shakespeare Quarterly*, x (1959) 3–9.

7. Ibid., p. 22. That there was not one but were several Tudor interpretations of the period from Richard II has been amply demonstrated in H. A. Kelly, *Divine Providence in the England of Shakespeare's Histories* (Cambridge, Mass., 1970).

8. Herbert Howarth, *The Tiger's Heart* (1970). J. W. Lever's 'Shakespeare and the Ideas of His Time', in *Shakespeare Survey 29* (Cambridge, 1976), provides a useful sketch of how much our notions about what Shakespeare and his age believed have changed in the last fifty years.

9. M. C. Bradbrook, *Themes and Conventions of Elizabethan Tragedy* (Cambridge, 1935); and Una Ellis-Fermor, *The Jacobean Drama* (1936).

10. Writing on Shakespeare's use of the disguise convention he points out, 'Viola's masquerade in *Twelfth Night* is scarcely to be reckoned a disguise, for it imposes on no one who knows her. Orlando in *As You Like It* has only once seen Rosalind in her proper shape, and so might not recognise her' – William Archer, *The Old Drama and the New* (1923) p. 42.

11. S. L. Bethell, *Shakespeare and the Popular Dramatic Tradition* (Durham, NC, 1944) p. 79.

12. John Palmer, *Political and Comic Characters of Shakespeare* (1962) pp. 184–5.

13. Daniel Seltzer, 'Prince Hal and Tragic Style', *Shakespeare Survey 30* (Cambridge, 1977) p. 23.

14. Ornstein, *A Kingdom for a Stage*, pp. 137–8.

15. J. F. Danby, *Shakespeare's Doctrine of Nature* (1948) pp. 96–7.

16. Derek Traversi, *Shakespeare from 'Richard II' to 'Henry V'* (1957) pp. 4, 58.

17. L. C. Knights, *Some Shakespearean Themes* (1959) pp. 23–4.

18. Ibid., pp. 52, 57–8.

19. *Dr Johnson on Shakespeare*, ed. W. K. Wimsatt (Harmondsworth, 1969) pp. 66, 107.

20. Christopher Spencer (ed.), *Five Restoration Adaptations of Shakespeare* (Urbana, Illinois, 1965) p. 253.

21. Knights, *Some Shakespearean Themes*, pp. 62–3.

22. T. J. B. Spencer, 'The Course of Shakespeare Criticism', *Shakespeare's World*, ed. James Sutherland and Joel Hurstfeld (1964) p. 170.

23. L. C. Knights, *Explorations* (1946) p. 16.

24. G. Wilson Knight, *The Wheel of Fire* (Oxford, 1930) p. 16.

25. F. R. Leavis referred darkly to 'the coterie crusade to re-impose Bradley' – *English Literature in Our Time and the University* (1969) p. 152. The truth is, as Katharine Cooke shows in *A. C. Bradley and his Influence in Twentieth-Century Shakespeare Criticism* (Oxford, 1972), that Bradley's influence was never wholly absent.

26. Ornstein, *A Kingdom for a Stage*, p. 129.

27. Knights, *Explorations*, p. 16.

28. *Dr Johnson on Shakespeare*, p. 120.

29. A. C. Bradley, *Oxford Lectures on Poetry* (1909) p. 273.

30. *Dr Johnson on Shakespeare*, pp. 117–18.

31. Bradley, *Oxford Lectures*, pp. 260, 263.

32. J. Dover Wilson, *The Fortunes of Falstaff* (Cambridge, 1943) pp. 18, 22.

33. Ornstein, *A Kingdom for a Stage*, p. 162.

34. II ii 63–5, II ii 477–81.

35. Wilson, *Fortunes of Falstaff*, p. 58.

36. Falstaff's frequent use of the 'if' construction was first noticed by Norman N. Holland in his excellent account of *Henry IV Part 1* in *The Shakespearean Imagination* (Bloomington, Ind., 1964). Falstaff's philosophical acceptance of life becomes less evident in *Part 2*, and both the attitude and the same speech patterns are given to Feeble in the recruiting scenes: 'I'll ne'er bear a base mind. An't be my destiny, so; an't be not, so. No man's too good to serve's Prince; and, let it go which way it will, he that dies this year is quit for the next' (III ii 228–32).

37. *Dr Johnson on Shakespeare*, p. 116.

38. Clifford Leech, 'The Unity of *2 Henry IV*', *Shakespeare Survey 6* (Cambridge, 1953) p. 24.

4 'THE TEMPEST'

1. E. E. Stoll, '*The Tempest*', *Publications of the Modern Language Association of America*, XLVII (1932) 699.

2. Lytton Strachey, *Books and Characters* (1922) p. 63.

3. L. L. Schücking, *Character Problems in Shakespeare's Plays* (1922) p. 243.

4. George Garrett and William Empson, *Shakespeare Survey* (1937) p. 55.

5. Ibid., pp. 42–3.

6. Colin Still, *The Timeless Theme* (1936); John Vyvyan, *The Shakespearean Ethic* (1959); J. E. Philips, '*The Tempest* and the Renaissance Idea of Man', *Shakespeare Quarterly*, xv (1964) 147–59; Frances A. Yates, *Shakespeare's Last Plays: A New Approach* (1975).

7. G. Wilson Knight, *The Crown of Life* (Oxford, 1947) p. 253.

8. F. D. Hoeniger, 'Prospero's Storm and Miracle', *Shakespeare Quarterly*, vii (1956) 33.

9. C. J. Sisson, 'The Magic of Prospero', *Shakespeare Survey 11* (Cambridge, 1958) p. 76.

10. Thomas McFarland, *Shakespeare's Pastoral Comedy* (Chapel Hill, NC, 1972) pp. 146, 174.

11. The fullest account of allegory in *The Tempest* is contained in A. D. Nuttall, *Two Concepts of Allegory: A Study of Shakespeare's 'The Tempest' and the Logic of Allegorical Expression* (1967). Nuttall concludes that the world of the play may be characterised as 'pre-allegorical'.

12. *The Tempest*, Penguin edn, ed. Anne Righter (Anne Barton) (Harmondsworth, 1968) p. 22.

13. Derek Traversi, *Shakespeare: The Last Phase* (1954) p. 194.

14. Ibid., p. 248.

15. *The Tempest*, New Arden edn, ed. Frank Kermode (1954) p. lxxxvii.

16. McFarland, *Shakespeare's Pastoral Comedy*, p. 164.

17. D. G. James, *The Dream of Prospero* (Oxford, 1968) p. 171.

18. In *Modern Shakespeare Offshoots* (Princeton, NJ, 1976) Ruby Cohn notes the interesting fact that '*The Tempest* is Shakespeare's last play to produce a flurry of offshoots, and they focus on Caliban rather than Prospero' (p. 267).

19. Howard Felperin, *Shakespearean Romance* (Princeton, NJ, 1972) p. 268.

20. W. Rockett, 'Labor and Virtue in *The Tempest*', *Shakespeare Quarterly*, xxiv (1973) 77.

21. Clifford Leech, *Shakespeare's Tragedies* (1950).

22. David William, '*The Tempest* on the Stage', in *Jacobean Theatre*, ed. John Russell Brown and Bernard Harris (1960) pp. 152–3.

23. William Empson, *The Structure of Complex Words* (1952) p. 123.

24. J. Middleton Murry, *Shakespeare* (1936) p. 395.

25. Douglas L. Peterson, *Time Tide and Tempest* (San Marino, Calif., 1973) p. 228.

26. R. A. Foakes, *Shakespeare: The Dark Comedies to the Last Plays* (1971) p. 164.

27. Robert Egan, *Drama Within Drama* (New York, 1975). The view was first advanced, to my knowledge, in K. M. Abenheimer, 'Shakespeare's *Tempest*: A Psychological Analysis', *Psycho-Analytic Review*, XXXIII (1946) 399–415. Since then it has been the subject of a few suggestive pages in David Horowitz, *Shakespeare: An Existential View* (1965), and Felperin, *Shakespearean Romance*.

28. F. W. Brownlow, *Two Shakespearean Sequences* (1977) p. 176. Brownlow's own view is that 'Prospero's aim is solely moral, justice for himself and his daughter, punishment for his enemies'; eventually, however, 'he abandons his whole design, except the betrothal of his daughter' (p. 179).

29. This would not be the first time in the play. See the exchange between Prospero and Miranda:

> MIRANDA   Sir, are not you my father?
> PROSPERO   Thy mother was a piece of virtue, and
>   She said thou wast my daughter . . . .   (I ii 55–7)

30. Ralph Berry, *The Shakespearean Metaphor* (1978) p. 111.

31. David Grene, *Reality and the Heroic Pattern* (Chicago, Ill., 1967) p. 95.

32. J. Conrad, *Lord Jim* (Harmondsworth, 1957) p. 163.

5 SHAKESPEARE: A SURVEY

1. T. S. Eliot, *On Poetry and Poets* (1957) p. 101.

2. Is it possible that there *is* some truth behind them? The conventional view says no. But we may be reluctant to dismiss Lucio's stories out of hand, partly on the time-honoured grounds that there is rarely smoke without fire, and partly because Lucio has already demonstrated a certain shrewdness of judgement about Angelo ('it is certain that when he makes water his urine is congeal'd ice' (III ii 101–3). Such a response may seem foolish or irresponsible. It is not, however, untheatrical. In John Barton's 1969 Stratford production the Duke was a wintry, lonely figure. Lucio's observation 'He had some feeling for the sport; he knew the service, and that instructed him to mercy' drew from him the startled denial 'I never *heard* the absent Duke much detected for

women' (ll. 110–14). His well-concealed secret is out. In this production
the Duke seemed to be a man in late middle age experiencing a recoil
from his sexually indulgent past. This conception made sense of his
previous failure to enforce the laws against illicit sex and his corresponding desire to see them enforced now. The fact that Lucio knew about his
guilty past and was obviously not the kind of character to keep silent
about it explains the vindictiveness of the Duke's attitude to him at the
end. Although Barnadine, a convicted murderer, is released, Lucio is
singled out as the 'one in place I cannot pardon' (v i 497), and he is
initially sentenced to flogging and hanging before being despatched to
marriage with Kate Keepdown.

3. Cf. the moment where Lear finds the right words to comfort the
blinded Gloucester:

> If thou wilt weep my fortunes, take my eyes.
> I know thee well enough; thy name is Gloucester.
> *Thou must be patient*; we came crying hither.
> Thou knowest the first time we smell the air
> We wawl and cry.   (IV vi 177–81)

6 CONCLUSION

1. What can be achieved in this way is well illustrated in Wilbur
Sanders and Howard Jacobson, *Shakespeare's Magnanimity* (1978). The
book has a polemical purpose, implicitly rejecting the form taken by
much present discussion of Shakespeare in favour of the approach
indicated by the subtitle, '*Four Tragic Heroes, Their Friends and
Families*'.

2. *Shakespeare Criticism: A Selection*, ed. D. Nichol Smith (Oxford,
1916) pp. 2, 6, 17, 48, 96–7.

3. Ibid., pp. 305–6, 344.

4. John Ruskin, *Modern Painters*, vol. IV (1856) p. 377.

5. Edmund Wilson, *The Triple Thinkers* (Harmondsworth, 1962)
p. 242.

6. Edward Dowden, *Shakespeare: A Critical Study of His Mind and Art*
(1875) p. xiii.

7. C. J. Sisson, 'The Mythical Sorrows of Shakespeare', *Proceedings of
the British Academy*, 1935.

8. Caroline Spurgeon, *Shakespeare's Imagery and What It Tells Us*
(Cambridge, 1935) pp. 204–5.

9. *The Letters of John Keats*, ed. M. Buxton Foreman, 2nd edn (Oxford, 1935) p. 72.

10. D. H. Lawrence, 'Thought', *Collected Poems*, ed. V. de Sola Pinto and F. Warren Roberts, vol. II (1964) p. 673.

11. Ernest Schanzer, *The Problem Plays of Shakespeare* (1963) p. 6.

12. E. A. J. Honigmann, *Shakespeare: Seven Tragedies* (1976) pp. 26–7.

13. Larry. S. Champion, *Shakespeare's Tragic Perspective* (Athens, Ga, 1976) p. 267.

14. Norman Rabkin, *Shakespeare and the Common Understanding* (New York, 1967) pp. 11–12.

15. Bernard McElroy, *Shakespeare's Mature Tragedies* (Princeton, NJ, 1973) pp. 9–10.

16. Philip Edwards, *Shakespeare and the Confines of Art* (1968) p. 162.

17. Howard Felperin, *Shakespearean Representation* (Princeton, NJ, 1977) p. 66.

18. Robert Grams Hunter, *Shakespeare and the Mystery of God's Judgements* (Athens, Ga, 1976) p. 2. One omission from this review of works with similarities both to each other and to my own argument has been *Shakespeare and the Story* by Joan Rees (1978). Mrs Rees's general approach and some of her actual conclusions are sufficiently close to mine to merit fuller reference than this brief note, but unfortunately her book did not come to hand until the present work was in proof.

19. Thomas McFarland, *Shakespeare's Pastoral Comedy* (Chapel Hill, NC, 1972) p. 171.

20. G. Wilson Knight, *The Imperial Theme*, 3rd edn (1951) p. 196.

21. D. J. Enright, 'Coriolanus: Tragedy or Debate?', *Essays in Criticism*, IV (1954) p. 19.

22. Schanzer, *Problem Plays*, p. 101.

23. Peter Brook, *The Open Space* (1968) p. 89.

24. Stanley Wells, *Royal Shakespeare* (Manchester, 1977) pp. 38–9. Although in my view the passage in question is open to both stated interpretations, it is only right to add that for Dr Wells the claim that Hamlet lapses into mere fatalism is a misreading of the play.

25. J. L. Styan, *The Shakespeare Revolution* (Cambridge, 1977). There is a stimulating account of some of Shakespeare's plays, drawing together the related contributions of critic, historian and director, in Alan C. Dessen, *Elizabethan Drama and the Viewer's Eye* (Chapel Hill, NC, 1977).

26. Jan Kott, *Shakespeare Our Contemporary* (1965).

27. For details of the cuts see Herbert S. Weil Jr, 'The Options of the

664

Audience: Theory and Practice in Peter Brook's *Measure for Measure*', *Shakespeare Survey 25* (Cambridge, 1972).

28. Kenneth McClellan documents the process with great liveliness and wit in *Whatever Happened to Shakespeare?* (1978).

29. John Russell Brown, *Free Shakespeare* (1974) p. 62.

Index

(Note: bold numerals refer to chapters.)